MS-DOS® QuickStart

2nd Edition

Developed by Que® Corporation

Text and graphics pages developed by
David W. Solomon and Lois Sherman

Revised for 2nd Edition by Michael Leventhal

CORPORATION
LEADING COMPUTER KNOWLEDGE
CARMEL, INDIANA

MS-DOS® QuickStart, 2nd Edition
Copyright © 1990 by Que® Corporation

Library of Congress Catalog No.: 90-62959

ISBN 0-88022-611-0

93 92 91 90   8 7 6 5 4 3 2 1

Interpretation of the printing code: the rightmost double-digit number is the year of the book's printing; the rightmost single-digit number, the number of the book's printing. For example, a printing code of 90-4 shows that the fourth printing of the book occurred in 1990.

This book can be used with DOS versions 4.01 and earlier.

Publishing Director

David Paul Ewing

Acquisitions Editor

Terrie Lynn Solomon

Product Director

Kathie-Jo Arnoff

Developmental Editor

Lois Sherman

Editor

Donald R. Eamon

Technical Editor

Andrew Young

Book Design and Production

William Hartman
Chuck Hutchinson
Betty Kish
Bob LaRoche
Dennis Sheehan
Denny Hager
Mary Beth Wakefield
Joe Ramon

Indexer

Sharon Hilgenberg

Composed in Garamond by

Hartman Publishing

Page Design and Production

William Hartman, Hartman Publishing

Table of Contents

Acknowledgments

Que Corporation thanks the following individuals for their contributions to the 2nd edition of this book:

Michael Leventhal, senior partner of Intercontinental Data Management, for making the text for the 2nd edition even more friendly and for making DOS less intimidating and easier to understand.

Kathie-Jo Arnoff, for her ongoing work on the development of the new QuickStart approach, for helping to restructure much of the material for this edition into the new format, and for guiding the author and editors throughout the project.

Lois Sherman, for her developmental work on both editions of this book, and particularly for her creativity in developing many of the conceptual illustrations.

Don Eamon, for his careful edit of the manuscript and for tracking the project from the original manuscript through the production process.

Andy Young, for his expert technical review of the text.

Bill Hartman, of Hartman Publishing, for his excellent design and layout of the pages and illustrations in this book.

David Solomon, for his technical expertise and talent, which he contributed to the 1st edition of this book.

Trademark Acknowledgments

Que Corporation has made every attempt to supply trademark information about company names, products, and services mentioned in this book. Trademarks indicated below were derived from various sources. Que Corporation cannot attest to the accuracy of this information.

1-2-3, Lotus, Lotus Freelance, and Symphony are registered trademarks of Lotus Development Corporation.

Amiga and Commodore are registered trademarks of Commodore Electronics, Ltd.

Andrew Tobias' Managing Your Money is a registered trademark of MECA (Micro Education Corporation of America).

Apple is a registered trademark of Apple Computer, Inc.

AST is a registered trademark of AST Research Inc.

Atari is a registered trademark of Atari Corporation.

AutoCAD is a registered trademark of Autodesk, Incorporated.

dBase IV and Map-Master are trademarks of Ashton-Tate Corporation.

COMPAQ is a registered trademark of COMPAQ Computer Corporation.

CP/M-80 is a registered trademark of Digital Research Inc.

Desk Jet is a trademark of Hewlett Packard Company

DeskMate is a registered trademark of Tandy Corporation.

Disk Optimizer is a registered trademark of SoftLogic Solutions Corporation.

EPSON is a registered trademark of Epson America, Inc.

First Publisher is a trademark of Software Publishing Corporation.

IBM, IBM PC, Personal Computer AT, and PS/2 are registered trademarks of International Business Machines Corporation.

Leading Edge is a registered trademark of Leading Edge Products, Inc.

Microsoft, MS-DOS, Microsoft Excel, and Flight Simulator are registered trademarks of Microsoft Corporation.

PageMaker is a registered trademark of Aldus Corporation.

PC-FILE is a trademark of Buttonware.

PC-Write is a registered trademark of Quick Soft.

Quattro, SideKick, and Reflex: The Analyst System are registered trademarks of Borland International, Inc.

Smart is a copyright of Innovative Software.

Introduction

This book describes the connection between personal computer hardware and the disk operating system and explains to beginning users all the most frequently used DOS commands. After you become familiar with DOS's commands and features, you can use the graphics presented here for quick reference.

Making Friends with DOS

DOS is easy! You've heard that statement before. It's the kind of glib remark that might make you wish for an adding machine and ball-point pen instead of a computer. Maybe you had a personal computer placed on your desk by a manager who "knows you can figure it out."

In a way, that's the worst rub because who wants to admit that they don't know where to begin? After all, your manager might conclude that you are not part of the high–tech generation. He or she might consider you an anachronism in the rapidly changing work place.

To add to the injury, perhaps everyone's eyes have shifted in your direction, secretly relieved that you— and not they—were chosen for the ordeal. Scanning your surroundings, your eyes focus on the gray cover of a thick book. It's the notorious DOS Manual, that coldly unemotional collection of cryptic commands, disjointed addendums, appendixes, suffixes, prefixes, and file listings.

As a young boy, I felt ambivalent about trips to the library. This was odd because I enjoyed reading, and I loved the feel of books in my small hands. Seeing row upon row of file cabinets filled with index cards, however, made my stomach tighten.

In time, I grew accustomed to the patronizing stares of bored librarians and the barbs of superiority from schoolmates. Although I long ago mastered the Dewey Decimal System, those wooden cabinets still make me a bit edgy.

Not that the system is incoherent or inconsistent: it isn't. In fact, the logic of the library system is remarkable. Nonetheless, the assumption that a logical system will be easy to learn simply because it is coherent and consistent is the ultimate in callousness.

Every day, thousands of intelligent Americans scratch their heads and berate themselves, feeling party to a multibillion dollar scam. After all, virtually everybody has been inundated by computer advertisements. You see ads in the newspapers, read mailings on sale items, hear about them from friends, and feel guilty about not learning how to use a computer.

Now, you've a new computer at your office, or you've decided that a PC will make working at home more efficient. Whatever the reason, you are now face–to–face with DOS.

What Is MS-DOS?

By itself, a computer is just a box and a screen. Ultimately, you're faced with the test of bringing it to life. This means mastering the computer's operating system, which for most of us is MS-DOS.

MS-DOS (or to most PC users, just *DOS*) is a tool you use to manage the information your computer stores in disk files. DOS is a collection of programs that form a foundation for you and your programs to work effectively with your computer. DOS is a set of standard routines that your programs use to access the services of the PC.

No matter what anybody tells you, the letters "D-O-S" do not stand for "Disheartening Obtuse Sadist." To make the most of your PC, you really have to understand its basics. Understanding DOS is required to enhance the enjoyment and productivity of running your microcomputer.

This book is an introduction to the most widely used *Disk Operating System* in the world. You will find that the material presented here is written in a unique manner. You won't be patronized with elementary definitions, and you won't be force-fed a litany of cryptic terms.

The microcomputer has gained respectability in the business world because of its ability to place technology directly in the hands of the people who most need that technology. As a result, the computer has automated both large and small businesses and boosted productivity in the office.

What Does This Book Contain?

Learning DOS can be enjoyable. *MS-DOS QuickStart,* 2nd Edition, is painless and worthwhile reading. Each chapter takes you on a guided tour of a specific part of DOS. You will be introduced to the concept of the MS-DOS and its straightforward, English-oriented commands.

At first you may feel like a spectator, but as you read each chapter, you will find the text fast-moving and the ideas presented in easy–to–understand graphics.

Chapter 1 describes the components of personal computer systems: the display, the keyboard, the system unit, and peripherals. The last part of Chapter 1 traces the way computers handle data.

Chapter 2 covers the fundamental concepts of how an operating system works. You will learn how to start—or boot—the computer in Chapter 3.

In Chapter 4, you learn important concepts about DOS commands: how to use a command name, to add parameters, and to edit and execute a command. Once you have learned the basics of issuing DOS commands, you are ready for Chapter 5, which covers preparing disks the computer can use.

Chapter 6 introduces hierarchical directories. This chapter clarifies the concept of hierarchy and explains the simple concept that lies behind DOS's method of hard disk organization.

In Chapter 7 you learn how to use the COPY command, which is the most frequently used—and the most misunderstood—DOS command. You also learn how to use the ERASE and RENAME commands.

Chapter 8, "Practicing Preventive Medicine," takes up the all-important topics of backing up disk files, computer hardware and software care, and avoiding data loss due to equipment failure.

Chapter 9 introduces a number of useful but little-used DOS commands. Among these are the redirection commands and such "workhorse" commands as TYPE and CHKDSK.

Chapter 10 covers batch files. Here, you discover that creating and using batch files is a matter of obeying a few simple rules.

For easy reference, Chapter 11 summarizes the most-used DOS commands. Chapter 12 lists common error messages you are likely to encounter as you use DOS and offers suggestions for dealing with each error.

An appendix covers DOS installation for both floppy disk and hard disk systems.

Finally, a detailed index helps you quickly find the information you need on a specific topic.

What Hardware Do You Need To Run MS-DOS?

The type of computer most likely to use MS-DOS is one that is compatible to a great extent with the International Business Machine Corporation's Personal Computer (IBM PC). COMPAQ, Zenith Data Systems, Tandy, Advanced Logic Research, AT&T, AST, EPSON, Wang, NEC, Toshiba, Sharp, Leading Edge, Hewlett-Packard, and many other companies manufacture or market MS-DOS based personal computers.

The computer should have at least 256 kilobytes (256K) of system random-access memory (RAM), at least one floppy disk drive, a display (screen), and a keyboard. These suggestions are minimal; most MS-DOS PCs sold today exceed these requirements.

For convenience and processing power, you may want to include a second floppy disk drive, a hard disk with at least 10 megabytes of storage capacity, a printer, and a color graphics display. You cannot use MS-DOS on most computers made by Apple Computer Inc., Commodore (except the newer

Amiga computers, when equipped with additional hardware), or Atari. These computers use operating systems that are sometimes referred to as DOS, but their operating systems are not MS-DOS compatible.

Conventions Used in This Book

Certain conventions are used throughout the text and graphics of *MS-DOS QuickStart*, 2nd Edition, to help you better understand the book's subject.

This book uses a symbolic form to describe command syntax. When you enter a command, you substitute real values for the symbolic name. Examples present commands that you can enter exactly as shown.

DOS commands can have various forms that are correct. For example, the syntax for the DIR command looks like this if you use symbolic names:

DIR *d:filename.ext* /W/P

DIR is the command name. The *d:filename.ext* is a symbolic example of a disk drive name and a file name. A real command would have actual values instead of symbols.

Some parts of a command are mandatory—required information needed by MS-DOS. Other command parts are optional. For the DIR command example, only the **DIR** is mandatory. The rest of the command, *d:filename /W/P*, is optional. When you enter only the mandatory command elements, DOS in many cases uses already-established values for the optional parts.

You can type upper- or lowercase letters in commands. DOS reads both as uppercase letters. You must type the syntax samples shown in this book letter-for-letter, but you can ignore case. Items shown in lowercase letters are variables. You type in the appropriate information for the items shown in lowercase.

In the example, the lowercase *d:* identifies the disk drive the command will use for its action. Replace the *d:* with A:, B:, or C:. The *filename.ext* stands for the name of a file, including its extension.

Spaces separate some parts of the command line. The slash separates other parts. The separators, or delimiter, are important to DOS because they help DOS break the command apart.

For example, typing **DIR A:** is correct; **DIRA:** is not.

Text that you are to type is displayed in **boldface**. Screen displays appear in this `special typeface`.

Keys are shown as they appear on the keyboard. The color blue emphasizes some of the more important areas of the graphics illustrations.

MS-DOS QuickStart, 2nd Edition,is your guide to becoming comfortable using DOS on your personal computer.

Understanding Computer Technology

Have you ever wondered why our society has emotional attachments for some machines, but not for others? We love our automobiles, for example, but we don't feel that way about refrigerators, or sinks, or our lawnmower.

I think the attachment to cars comes from our capacity to develop a very interactive relationship with a mechanical beast. We are social creatures, and not many mechanical contraptions supply us with that give and take we seem to need. That may be why we have such love affairs with those that do.

One contraption most of us love is a VCR with a remote control. With a VCR's remote, you can feel in control as it responds at the click of a command. You can control its speed, sound, and a host of other ego-related factors.

A personal computer is another machine that provides an abundance of emotional "bang for the buck"—for some. Other people, including you, may be like I was. When I purchased my first microcomputer, I was disappointed. It appeared to be little more than a big dumb box. In fact, if I hadn't needed it for business, I would have preferred a new color television.

1

Key Terms in This Chapter

Display   The screen or monitor.

Peripheral   Any device, aside from the computer itself, that either lets you do something or shows the results. A good example of a peripheral is your printer.

Disk   A plastic or metal platter coated with magnetic material, used to store files. A *disk drive* records and plays back information on disks. Disks resemble small phonograph records. Like the arm of a phonograph, the read/write head swings into position over the spinning disk to retrieve data.

Modem   A device for exchanging data between computers through standard telephone lines. All information transfers via computer-generated audio signals.

Input   Any data given to a computer.

Output   Any data transmitted by a computer.

Bit   A binary digit. The smallest discrete representation of a value a computer can manipulate. A computer thinks only in numbers. Bits are similar to the dot/dash concept used in Morse code.

Byte   A collection of eight bits that a computer usually stores and manipulates as a full character (letter, number, or symbol). A byte is a character identified by a sequence of numbers.

K (kilobyte)   1024 bytes, used to show size or capacity in computer systems. Technically, the term *kilo* means thousand, but allow the computer revolution its poetic license.

M (megabyte)   1000 kilobytes. Used to measure values or capacities greater than 999K.

Data   A catchall term meaning words, numbers, symbols, graphics, or sounds. Data is any information stored in computer byte form.

File   A named group of data in electronic form. In word processing, a file could be a letter. In a database system, a file could be a name and address list.

1

Right now, you too might prefer to be doing something else. But you need to learn how to use a personal computer. You may be anxious about getting started, but believe me when I tell you that if you understand something about how the contraption works, you will feel a good deal better about learning to use it. This chapter provides a quick but illuminating lesson about how microcomputers work. Learning about the personal computer, its components, and how all the parts work together is like learning new car controls: displays and keyboards (dashboards), the CPU (engine control unit), peripherals (tires), and disk drives (the cassette player).

Does a computer take you from zero to sixty in six seconds? Even faster: it takes you to the speed of light. Computers may not yet turn you into an Indy car driver, but you'll be capable of participating in a drama of your own making.

This chapter explains the components that have become a standard for the IBM PC and compatibles. Do you need to remember every term you read? Not unless you're a college student preparing for a final exam. Nevertheless, this chapter's design will help you enjoy working with your new computer. After all, it's always useful to know where the oil goes in your car. And as cars and VCRs have their own terminology, so does the microcomputer.

Every term defined here is rooted in the English language. These terms are no more mysterious than such terms as *dashboard*, *acceleration*, *mileage*, *pause*, *reverse*, or *freeze-frame*. Computer terms are simple to remember and impressive at the office. Knowing them may even get you a raise.

Understanding Computer Technology

Until a few years ago computers were large, expensive machines generally unavailable to individual users. The rich could afford them, but who wanted to fill three rooms of his home with energy-guzzling electronics that served no practical purpose?

Advances in computer technology led to the engineering of smaller computer parts called *chips*. Most of the essential information and circuitry a computer needs resides on one of these chips, called the *microprocessor*. This capability means a savings in both space and energy. The ultimate product of chip technology is your *microcomputer*.

In the early 1980s, International Business Machines (IBM) introduced the Personal Computer. Whether or not the PC is the best of the breed is

9

1

arguable, but IBM gave microcomputers respectability in the business community. As a leader in the large business computer market, IBM held an excellent marketing position. IBM's name, sales force, and corporate contacts made the PC today's standard in home and business computing. The arrival of the Personal Computer worked out well. IBM created both a market for PCs and a standard upon which other firms have built.

Today, many manufacturers produce computers that are in many ways superior to the IBM product line. Rapid technical developments in newly created companies raised microcomputer technology to new heights. Even the venerable IBM uses much of this technology in its newest PCs.

These "PC clones" were dubbed *compatibles*, and the intense competition between these computers and IBM benefits everybody. Never before could you purchase so much computing power at such a reasonable price.

A computer system is composed of hardware parts that exist in a variety of configurations. All MS-DOS computers operate in essentially the same manner.

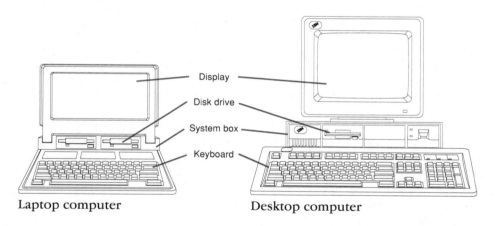

Laptop computer   Desktop computer

Defining the PC

Engineers base the size of the computer more on human physiology than on anything else. Designers developed the standard model to be large enough to contain disk drives and other devices. The laptop, on the other hand, is designed to be small and light, perfect for computing while on the road.

1

Whether your system is an IBM or a compatible model, your PC is engineered for both comfort and convenience.

Components of Computer Systems

Personal computer systems based on the IBM PC are functionally the same, despite the wide variety of configurations available. As long as you have the main components, the shape and size of your computer matter very little. For example, you can find equally powerful machines in the traditional desktop configuration, in portable laptop models, or in compact lunchbox-sized computers. The wide variety of PC software operates equally well in any of these cosmetic configurations.

Hardware and Software

Hardware and software make up the two main segments of a computer system. Both must be present for a computer to work. Many texts waste several pages supplying nonsense definitions for terms that are simple, but this book won't.

Hardware refers to the physical machine and its peripherals—electronics and moving parts of metal and plastic. Your VCR, television, tape deck, CD, and turntable are also hardware.

Software encompasses the program and data files created, stored, and run by your PC. These records are the equivalent of text books, novels, newspapers, and videotapes. Table 1.1 illustrates the variety of software available for your computer.

The *operating system* provides the working base for all other programs. It creates a uniform means for programs to gain access to the full resources of the hardware. Operating systems that help programs to access disks are called *disk operating systems*, or DOS.

This book covers the common operating system for IBM PC compatibles: MS-DOS. The IBM versions of DOS and the various versions of Microsoft Corporation's DOS are highly compatible. Actually, they're nearly identical, except that IBM calls its version PC-DOS, whereas Microsoft calls its version MS-DOS. For this reason, *DOS* is used in this text as the generic term when referring to both packages.

1

Table 1.1
Computer Software

Type of software	Examples
Operating systems	MS-DOS (See Chapter 2); UNIX
Databases	dBASE IV; Reflex: The Analyst; PC-FILE
Spreadsheets	Lotus 1-2-3; SuperCalc; Quattro Pro
Word processors	WordPerfect; WordStar; PC-WRITE
Utilities	SideKick; DeskMate (calendar, notepad, calculator)
Graphics	AutoCAD; Map Master; Lotus Freelance Plus
Integrated programs	Smart; Symphony
Games	Flight Simulator
Home finance	Managing Your Money
Desktop publishing	First Publisher; Ventura Publisher; PageMaker

Text and Graphics Displays

The video *display* (also called the monitor or screen) describes the part of the computer's hardware that produces visual images. To date, the cathode ray tube (CRT) type of monitor, which operates on the same principle as a television set, provides the crispest, most easily read image.

On the display, a blinking symbol (box, underscore, or other character) shows where the next character appears. This symbol is the *cursor*.

```
Current date is Fri 10-12-1990
Enter new date (mm-dd-yy):
Current time is  1:19:50.87p
Enter new time:

IBM DOS Version 4.00
        (C)Copyright International Business Machines Corp 1981, 1988
        (C)Copyright Microsoft Corp 1981-1986

A> ▄
```

12

Computers are visually graphic in that they try to let you know what they are doing. They also prefer that you be the boss. That's why the video display is the normal, or *default*, location the computer uses to communicate with you. Manufacturers also incorporate other types of technology into computer displays. For example, to build flatter displays, manufacturers use a technology known as gas plasma. Gas plasma displays produce an orange color against a dark background. This type of display is found primarily in portable computers, where a TV-type display would be heavy and cumbersome.

Another technology adapted to computer displays is liquid crystal. Liquid crystal displays (LCDs) work on the same principle as today's digital watch displays. Most LCDs produce dark characters against a lighter background.

LCDs work well in brightly lit rooms, because the light striking the display increases the contrast of the display image. Some LCDs also use a backlight to increase the display's contrast. Again, this type of display appears primarily on portables.

Regardless of the display type, all computer screens take electrical signals and translate them into patterns of tiny dots, or *pixels*, an acronym coined from the phrase, *picture element*. You can recognize pixels as characters or figures. The more pixels a display contains, the sharper the visual image. The sharpness of the image is its *resolution*.

The higher-resolution image (left) uses four times as many pixels as the lower-resolution image (right).

The resolution of the visual image is a function of both the display and the *display adapter*. The display adapter controls the computer display. In some PCs the display circuitry is a part of the motherboard (see this chapter's section "The System Unit and Peripherals"). The display adapter can also reside on a separate board that fits into a slot in the computer. The display adapter can be a monochrome display adapter (MDA), color graphics adapter (CGA), enhanced graphics adapter (EGA), video graphics array adapter (VGA), or other less common display adapter.

1

Text Display

When you see letters, numbers, or punctuation on your display, you recognize these images as text. This text comes from your computer's memory where the text has been stored under the standard that most computers recognize, the American Standard Code for Information Interchange (ASCII). Each ASCII code represents a letter or a symbol. These codes are sent to the display adapter so you can see the characters on the screen. Because ASCII is the industry standard, the display adapter uses an electronic table to pull the correct pixel pattern for any letter, number, or punctuation symbol.

You will see occasional references to *extended* ASCII codes. This means that the ASCII-to-pixel table can have 256 different combinations, more than enough to represent all letters, numbers, and punctuation. Display adapters use the leftover ASCII values for patterns of lines, corners, and special images, such as musical notes.

In fact, 128 ASCII values remain for these special images. Programs can use combinations of these extended ASCII characters to produce boxes and other graphics-like characters. However, if a program needs to display a pixel or pattern of pixels not included in the ASCII-to-pixel table, you are out of luck. Text adapters cannot generate special graphics characters. Of the various display adapters available, only the monochrome display adapter (MDA) is a text-only display adapter.

Graphics Display

Graphics displays can produce any pixel, or pattern of pixels. This type of display lets you view, on-screen, complex figures with curves and fine detail. The computers work harder to create graphics images than text images, however, because images are "painted" on the screen with pixels. To light the correct point on the display, the display adapter must find the screen coordinate points for each pixel. Unlike text mode, no table of predetermined pixels exists for graphics mode.

Graphics displays differ in the number of pixels available. The greater the number of pixels, the finer the detail of the display. Each pixel contains characteristics that describe to the graphics adapter what the color or intensity of the pixel should be. The greater the number of colors and intensities, the more storage space in memory you need. Graphics adapters offer varying combinations of pixel density, number of colors, and intensity.

Table 1.2 lists the various display types, showing pixel number and resolution, and the colors available with each type of display adapter.

Table 1.2
Resolution and Colors for Display Adapters

Adapter Type	Graphics Mode	Pixel Resolution	Colors Available
CGA	Medium resolution	320 × 200	4
CGA	High resolution	640 × 200	2
EGA	All CGA modes		
EGA	CGA high resolution	640 × 200	16
EGA	EGA high resolution	640 × 350	16
MGA	Monochrome graphics	720 × 348	2
MDA	Text ONLY	N/A	N/A
VGA	All CGA modes		
VGA	All EGA Modes		
VGA	Monochrome	640 × 480	2
VGA	VGA high resolution	640 × 480	16
VGA	VGA Medium resolution	320 × 200	256
EVGA	EVGA high resolution	800 × 600	256
Super VGA	Super VGA very high resolution	1024 × 768	16

Keyboards

Like a typewriter, a computer keyboard contains all the letters of the alphabet. The numbers, symbols, and punctuation characters are virtually the same. The computer keyboard has the familiar QWERTY layout. The term *QWERTY* comes from the letters found on the left side of the top row of keys on a standard typewriter. However, a computer keyboard differs from a typewriter keyboard in several important ways.

1

The keyboard is one way you put information into the computer. The computer then converts every character you type into code the machine can understand. The keyboard is therefore an *input device*.

The most notable differences are the extra keys that do not appear on a typewriter. These keys are described in table 1.3. Also, depending on the type of computer you use, you will see 10 or 12 special *function keys*.

Table 1.3
Special Keys on the Computer Keyboard

	Key	Function
↵Enter	Enter	Signals the computer to respond to the commands you type. Also functions as a carriage return in programs that simulate the operation of a typewriter.
←, →, ↓, ↑	Cursor keys	Changes your location on the screen. Included are the arrow, PgUp, PgDn, Home, and End keys.
←Backspace	Backspace	Moves the cursor backward one space at a time, deleting any character in that space.
Del	Delete	Deletes, or erases, any character at the location of the cursor.
Ins	Insert	Inserts any character at the location of the cursor.
⇧Shift	Shift	Enables you to capitalize letters when you hold down Shift while you type the letter. When pressed in combination with another key, Shift can change the standard function of that key.
Caps Lock	Caps Lock	When pressed to the lock position, all characters typed are uppercase, or capitalized. Caps Lock doesn't shift the numbered keys, however. To release, press the key again.
Ctrl	Control	When pressed in combination with another key, changes the standard function of that key.

16

Table 1.3—(continued)

	Key	Function
Alt	Alternate	When pressed in combination with another key, changes the standard function of that key.
Esc	Escape	In some situations, allows you to escape from a current operation to a previous one. Sometimes Esc has no effect on the current operation.
Num Lock	Number Lock	Changes the numeric pad from cursor-movement to numeric-function mode.
PrtSc	Print Screen	Key found on AT Keyboards. Used with the Shift key to send the characters on the display to the printer.
PrtSc	Print Screen	Key found on Enhanced Keyboards. Same as PrtSc.
Scroll Lock	Scroll Lock	Locks the scrolling function to the cursor-movement keys. Instead of the cursor's moving, the screen scrolls.
Pause	Pause	Suspends display activity until you press another key. (Not provided with standard keyboards.)
Break	Break	Stops a program in progress from running.
7 8 9 / 4 5 6 / 1 2 3 / 0 .	Numeric keypad	A cluster of keys to the right of the standard keyboard. The keypad includes numbered keys from 0 to 9 as well as cursor-movement keys and other special keys.

Many of the function keys are designed for use in combination with other keys (see table 1.4). For example, pressing the Shift and PrtSc keys in combination causes DOS to print the contents of the current screen. Holding down the Ctrl key while pressing the PrtSc key causes DOS to continuously print what you type. Pressing Ctrl and PrtSc a second time turns off the printing.

1

The *function keys* are shortcuts. Not all programs use these keys, and some use only a few of them. When used, however, they automatically carry out certain operations for you. For example, programs often use the F1 key for *on-line help*. On-line help displays instructions from the computer's memory to help you understand a particular operation. The DOS V4.0 shell uses the F3 key to back out of one operation and move into another. The F10 key moves the cursor to various parts of the screen.

Table 1.4
DOS Key Combinations

Keys	Function
Ctrl-S	Freezes the display. Pressing Ctrl-Q or any other key restarts the display.
Ctrl-PrtSc	Sends lines to both the screen and to the printer; pressing this sequence a second time turns off this function.
Ctrl-C or Ctrl-Break	Stops the execution of a program.
Ctrl-Alt-Del	Restarts MS-DOS (system reset).

The standard keyboard comes with keys F1 through F10 on the left side. The Extended keyboard offers keys F1 through F12 across the top of the keys in all except one brand of keyboard. This Extended keyboard must have been designed by programmers. These people are known for being poor typists and this keyboard layout is the result. On the other hand, the Extended keyboard offers more options.

AT and Enhanced Keyboards

Many early PC-compatible computers use a standard keyboard design similar to that of the IBM PC. Other machines use a Personal Computer AT-style keyboard. The new IBM PS/2 computers use a 101-key Enhanced Keyboard. Some users prefer the layout of the standard keyboard, and others prefer the Enhanced Keyboard.

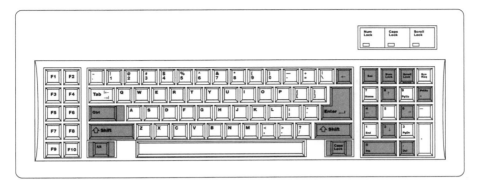

AT keyboard

You can determine whether your computer has a standard keyboard, a
Personal Computer AT-style keyboard, or an Enhanced Keyboard. You find
certain keys only on specific keyboards. For example, you find the Print
Screen and Pause keys only on the Enhanced Keyboard. You can, however,
simulate these keys by using a combination of keys on the standard
keyboard.

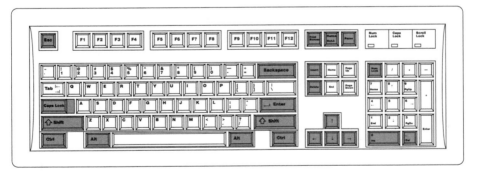

Enhanced keyboard

The 102-Key Keyboards

Some new keyboards allow you to change key caps and switch key
definitions for the Caps Lock, Ctrl, Esc, and tilde (~) keys. Northgate
Computer Systems, for example, not only offers these options, but also

provides an enhanced keyboard. The enhanced keyboard locates the first 10 functions keys to the left instead of across the top of the alphabet and number keys. The layout requires one more key than a 101-key enhanced keyboard—thus the 102-key keyboard.

Nonstandard Keyboards

Small "lunchbox" and portable laptop computers employ nonstandard keyboards, usually to conserve space. A few of these computers have so little keyboard space that you may need to add an external numeric keypad for software that manipulates numbers.

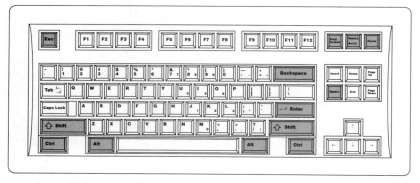

Space-saver keyboard

If your PC came with the standard F1 through F10 keys and your friend's keyboard has 12, don't feel cheated. The standard keyboard is better for people involved in text-intensive work. Triggering a word processing command with your left pinkie is a snap because your fingers rarely have to leave the home keys. Also, the standard keyboard has a larger Enter key, and quick fingers don't plunge into plastic valleys.

The System Unit and Peripherals

Industry engineers designed the standard desktop PC around a box-shaped cabinet that connects to all other parts of the computer. This box is called the *system unit*. The devices attached to it are *peripherals*. The system unit and the peripherals complete the hardware portion of the computer system.

20

The System Unit

The system unit houses all but a few parts of a PC. Included are various circuit boards, a power supply, and even a small speaker. System units vary in appearance, but a horizontal box shape is the most common. A vertical tower shape is becoming popular because it frees desk or table space.

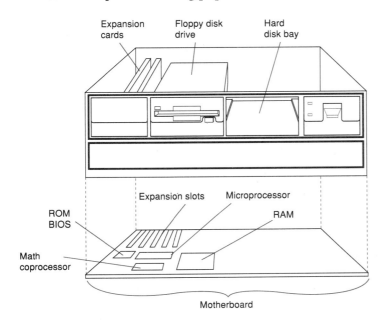

A hypothetical system unit, showing the placement of the hard and floppy disk drives and the system board, also called the motherboard.

The motherboard holds the main electronic components of the computer. The microprocessor, the chips that support it, and various other circuits are the primary parts on the motherboard. Normally, there are electrical sockets on the motherboard where you can plug in various adapter circuit boards. These electrical sockets are called *expansion slots*.

Chips that provide the computer with its memory are located on the motherboard. In some cases, you can plug an additional memory adapter into an available expansion slot to increase the system's memory. The number of available expansion slots varies with each PC builder. Most motherboards have a socket for a math coprocessor. Math coprocessors help speed up programs that manipulate large volumes of graphics or math equations. Spreadsheet programs and desktop publishing software, for example, benefit from the addition of a math coprocessor chip.

1 Disk Drives and Disks

Disk drives are complex mechanisms that carry out a fairly simple function: they rotate *disks*, circular platters or pieces of plastic that have magnetized surfaces. As the disk rotates, the drive converts electrical signals from the computer and places the information into or retrieves information from magnetic fields on the disk. The storage process is called *writing* data to the disk. Disk drives also recover, or *read*, magnetically stored data and present it to the computer as electrical signals. You don't lose magnetically stored data when the computer's power is off.

The components of a disk drive are similar to those of a phonograph. The disk, like a record, rotates. A positioner arm, like a tone arm, moves across the radius of the disk. A head, like a pickup cartridge, translates information into electrical signals. Unlike phonographs, disk drives do not have spiral grooves on the disk's surface. The disk's surface is recorded in magnetic, concentric rings, or *tracks*. The tighter these tracks are packed on the disk, the greater the storage capacity of the disk.

Computers use both sides of a disk for encoding information. Most computers operate in this manner; that's why these computers are called *double-sided* disk drive systems.

When computers write to the disk, they store groups of data that the operating system identifies as *files*. You can tell that a drive is reading or writing when the small light on the front of the disk drive glows. You should never open a drive door or eject a disk until the light goes out, unless the computer specifically instructs you to do so.

Two types of disks are available, in a variety of data storage capacities. Disks are either *floppy* or *hard*. Floppy disks are removable, flexible, and of a lower capacity than hard disks. Hard disks, also called *fixed* disks, are usually high-capacity rigid platters that can't be removed as floppies can.

Hard disks are sealed inside the hard disk drive. Floppy disks are encased in flexible 5 1/4-inch jackets or in rigid 3 1/2-inch jackets.

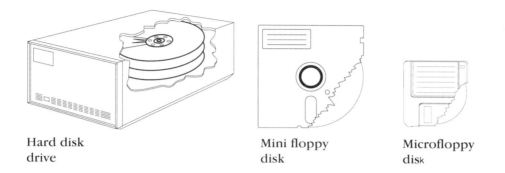

Hard disk
drive

Mini floppy
disk

Microfloppy
disk

Floppy Disks

Floppy disks store from 360K to 1.44M bytes of data. They come in two
common sizes. *Minifloppies* are 5 1/4-inch disks, and *microfloppies* are 3 1/2-
inch disks. The measurement refers to the size of the disk's jacket. Unless
size is important, this book simply refers to both disk types as *floppies*.

Make sure that you know your drive's specification before you buy or
interchange floppies. Floppies of the same size, but with different capacities,
can be incompatible with a particular disk drive.

A high density disk drive, for example, can format, read, and write to both
high density and double-density floppy disks. A double-density disk drive can
only use double-density disks.

Fixed Disks

Hard disks often consist of multiple, rigid-disk platters. The platters spin at
3,600 RPM, much faster than a floppy disk drive spins. As the platters spin
within the drive, the head positioners make small, precise movements above
the tracks of the disk. Because of this precision, hard disks can store
enormous quantities of data—from 10M to more than 100M. Despite the
precision of hard disks, they are reasonably rugged devices. Factory sealing
prevents contamination of the housing. With proper care, hard disks can
deliver years of trouble-free service.

Hard disks range from 3 1/2 to 8 inches in diameter. The most common size,
5 1/4 inches, holds between 2 1/2 and 10 megabytes of information per side.

1

Peripherals

Besides the display and the keyboard, a variety of peripherals can be useful to you. Peripherals such as a mouse, printer, modem, joystick, and digitizer let you more easily communicate with your computer. For example, using a mouse with a modern computer program—such as a desktop publishing package—takes best advantage of the program's features.

The Mouse

The mouse is an input device that moves on the surface of your work space and causes the computer to correlate this movement to the display. The mouse is shaped to fit comfortably under your hand. The contour and the cable that trails from the unit gives the vague appearance of a mouse sitting on the table. The mouse has one, two, or three buttons that rest beneath the fingers of the operator's hand.

Not all software supports a mouse, but many popular programs do. Many mouse-based programs let you point to options on the display and click a mouse button to carry out a task.

A mouse is a computer input device whose shape vaguely resembles that of a real mouse.

A joystick is popular for use in games and is used to enter information into the computer. Often, joysticks replace keyboard operations.

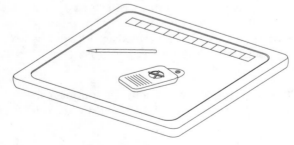

For many users, a digitizer tablet feels more natural than using a mouse. When a digitizer's "puck" moves across the tablet, that motion is displayed on-screen.

1

Printers

Printers accept signals (*input*) from the CPU and convert those signals to characters (*output*), usually imprinted on paper. You can classify printers in the following ways:

- By the way they receive input from the computer
- By how they produce output

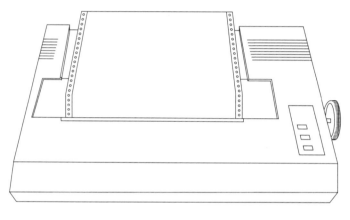

A printer can be thought of as a typewriter without a keyboard. It accepts data from the computer and renders it as characters on paper.

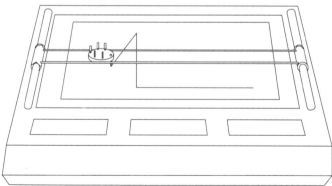

A plotter lets you draw with the computer. Unlike the printer, a plotter draws up and down as well as back and forth.

You connect printers to the system unit through a *port*. A port is an electrical doorway through which data flows between the system unit and an outside peripheral. A port has its own expansion adapter or shares an expansion adapter with other ports or circuits, such as a CGA card.

1

The terms *parallel* and *serial* describe two types of ports that send output from personal computers to printers. A parallel port continuously sends all the bits of data synchronously, through separate wires in the cable, one byte (character) at a time. Parallel printer connections are more common than serial connections. A serial port delivers the bits of data, one byte after another, in single-file fashion. Although sending one complete byte (character) by using serial communications takes longer, serial ports require fewer wires in the cable. Serial printers also can communicate with the port over longer distances than parallel printers.

All printers have the job of putting their output onto paper. Often, this output is text, but it also may be graphics images. Three major classifications of printers (*dot-matrix*, *daisywheel*, and *laser*) exist. Each printer type produces characters in unique ways. Printers are usually rated by their printing speed and the quality of the finished print. Some printers print by using all the addressable points on the screen, much as a graphics display adapter does. Some printers produce color prints.

Of late, another type of printer has been growing in popularity. The ink jet printer (such as the Hewlett Packard DeskJet) literally sprays words and graphics on a page in near-silence. Moderately priced, the DeskJet's print quality rivals that of a laser printer, and of all the printers, only a laser is faster and sharper than this high-resolution printer.

The most common printer, the dot-matrix, uses a print head that contains a row of pins or wires to produce the characters. A motor moves the print head horizontally across the paper. As the print head moves, a vertical slice of each character forms as the printer's controlling circuits fire the proper pins. The wires press corresponding small dots of the ribbon against the paper, leaving an inked dot impression. After several tiny horizontal steps, the print head leaves the dot image of a complete character. The process continues for each character on the line.

The daisywheel printer also steps the print head across the page, but produces a complete character for each step. The characters of the alphabet are arranged at the ends of "petals" that resemble spokes on a wheel. The visual effect of this wheel is similar to a daisy's petals arranged around the flower head. Because the daisywheel prints fully-formed characters, the quality of daisywheel printing is high. Daisywheel printers are far slower than dot-matrix printers and are becoming obsolete.

Laser printers use a technology that closely resembles that of photocopying. Instead of a light-sensitive drum picking up the image of an original, the drum is painted with the light of a laser diode. The image on the drum transfers to the paper in a high dot density output. With high dot density, the printed characters look fully formed. Laser printers also can produce graphics image output. The high-quality text and graphics combination is useful for desktop publishing.

Modems

A modem is a peripheral that helps your PC communicate with other computers over standard telephone lines. Modems are serial communications peripherals. They send or receive characters or data one bit at a time. Most modems communicate with other modems at speeds ranging from 300 to 9600 bps, or bits per second. Modems need special communications software to coordinate data exchanges with other modems.

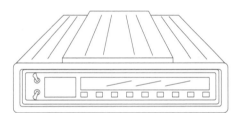

A modem transfers signals between computers by using telephone lines.

How Computers Work with Data

Now that you have learned about the essential parts of the computer system, you are ready for an overview of how all these parts carry out the job of computing. The world inside a computer is a strange place. Fortunately, you do not have to know the details of a computer's operation to produce finished work. However, if you explore a little bit, you will adjust more quickly to using your computer.

Computers perform many useful tasks by accepting data as input, processing it, and releasing it as output. Data is information. It can be a set of numbers, a memo, an arrow key that moves a game symbol, or anything you can imagine.

The computer translates input into electrical signals that move through a set of electronic controls. Output can be thought of in four ways:

- As characters the computer displays on the screen
- As signals the computer holds in its memory
- As signals stored magnetically on disk
- As permanent images and graphics printed on paper

Computers receive and send output in the form of electrical signals. These signals are stable in two states: on and off. Think of these states as you would electricity to a light switch that you can turn on and off. Computers contain millions of electronic switches that can be either on or off. All input and output follows this two-state principle.

Binary, the computer name for the two-state principle, consists of signals that make up true computer language. Computers interpret data as two binary digits, or *bits*—0 and 1. For convenience, computers group eight bits together. This eight-bit grouping, or *byte*, is sometimes packaged in two-, four-, or eight-byte packages when the computer moves information internally.

Computers move bits and bytes across electrical highways called *buses*. Normally, the computer contains three buses: the *control bus*, the *data bus*, and the *address bus*. The microprocessor connects to all three buses and supervises their activity. The CPU uses the data bus to determine *what* the data should be, the control bus to confirm *how* the electrical operations should proceed, and the address bus to determine *where* the data is to be positioned in memory.

Because the microprocessor can call on this memory at any address, and in any order, it is called *random-access memory*, or *RAM*. The CPU reads and executes program instructions held in RAM. Resulting computations are stored in RAM.

Some computer information is permanent. This permanent memory, called *read-only memory* (or *ROM*), is useful for holding unalterable instructions in the computer system.

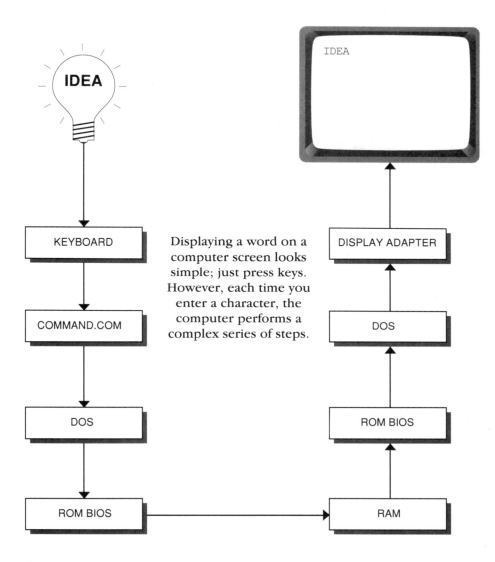

Displaying a word on a computer screen looks simple; just press keys. However, each time you enter a character, the computer performs a complex series of steps.

The microprocessor depends on you to give it instructions in the form of a *program*. A program is a set of binary-coded instructions that produces a desired result. The microprocessor decodes the binary information and carries out the instruction from the program.

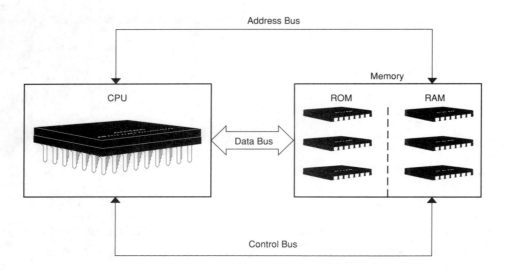

You could start from scratch and type programs or data into the computer every time you turn on the power. Of course, you don't want to do that if you don't have to. Luckily, the computer stores both instructions and start-up data, usually on a disk. Disks store data in binary form in *files*. To the computer, a file is just a collection of bytes identified by a unique name. These bytes can be a memo, a word processing program, or some other program. A file's function is to hold binary data or programs safely until you type a command on the keyboard to direct the microprocessor to call for that data or program file. When the call comes, the drive reads the file and writes its contents into RAM.

Lessons Learned

■ The PC revolution is no more difficult to understand than the home video revolution. MS-DOS and your microcomputer are about to unlock a new dimension in entertainment and productivity.

■ If you feel comfortable with a computer, you can accept and enjoy all that goes with it, just like you can your VCR.

■ The PC on your table or desk is a product of years of development and more than one company's efforts.

■ Computer terminology is simple. The words are basic, and the definitions are easy to understand.

■ Hardware, software, screen displays, keyboards, disks, drives, mice, modems, and memory are the tools of microcomputer technology.

Now, let's talk about learning your computing ABCs.

1

Learning Your DOS ABCs

Although I was very young, I will always remember my first day at kindergarten. Despite my mother's reassuring hand, I walked down those unfamiliar corridors with a stomach that churned like a mass of oatmeal.

Slowly, we entered the classroom to meet my new teacher. Worse, she was my first teacher. Back then, the word "teacher" conjured up an image of the Wicked Witch of the West from *The Wizard of Oz*. Children often see new authority figures as frightening, all-powerful people. Being small and vulnerable in strange surroundings, a child is already insecure. This feeling increases as the parent leaves the classroom. I was afraid of the unknown.

You can't escape the unknown. You face it whenever you reach out to gain knowledge or to experience new events. Some people skydive; others camp out in unfamiliar wilderness. Many people, perhaps including you, enjoy the safer mental stimulation from movies of various genres.

So, as you stare at your new microcomputer and flip through your DOS manual, you need not fear that the computer screen will dissolve into a churning fog and then clear to reveal the Wicked Witch of the West.

2

Key Terms Used in This Chapter

Program	Instructions that tell a computer what to do and how to do it.
BIOS	Basic Input/Output System. The software that performs basic communications between the computer and the peripherals.
Redirection	A change in the source or destination that is normally used for input and output.
Applications programs	Instructions that tell the computer to perform a program-specific task, such as word processing. It's a "how to" for the computer.
Interface	A connection between parts of the computer, particularly between hardware devices. Also, the interaction between you and an applications program.
Batch file	A series of DOS commands placed in a disk file. DOS executes batch-file commands one at a time. You might call batch files the "nonprogrammer's programs."

Computers can add a new and pleasurable dimension to your life. Believe it or not, the classic "hero" and friend who helps you through this fear of the unknown is the *disk operating system*, or *DOS*. DOS is a product of ingenuity. At first, it may feel distant and overpowering, but many heroes present that image.

Chapter 1 covered software, mechanics, computer systems, and component parts. This chapter introduces DOS, the most important link between hardware, other software, and you. It brings DOS closer to you by defining the disk operating system, its uses, and its interesting history. After all, even heroes have a past.

An operating system is a collection of computer programs that provides recurring services to other programs and to the user of a computer. DOS unleashes the potential of your computer by translating into action, through commands, your desire to manipulate data.

2

If you think of the computer hardware as a theater's empty stage, and an applications program as an ongoing play, you can see a void between them. There is a lot of support behind the "scenes."

Operating system software does the computer-equivalent job of the set-preparation crews, the lighting crews, the stage hands, the makeup artist, and even the janitor. All the services that must bridge the gap between the hardware and a user's program are performed by the operating system software. The program is not burdened with routine details. Can you imagine the lead actress having to push her own backdrop onto the stage just before the curtain goes up?

Imagine yourself as the producer/director. You have full control over the stage (hardware) and stage crew (operating system), and what plays (applications programs) you will produce. You now have a good idea where you fit into the production.

If a computer's operating system did not supply these services, you would have to deal directly with the details of controlling the hardware. Without the disk operating system, for example, every computer program would have to hold *instructions* telling the hardware each step to take to do its job.

Because operating systems already contain instructions, you or a program can call on DOS to control your computer. Disk operating systems get their name from the attention given to the disks in the computer system.

IBM-compatible personal computers use MS-DOS, the disk operating system developed (though not invented) by Microsoft Corporation. Manufacturers of personal computers—such as Zenith, IBM, and COMPAQ—modify MS-DOS for their computers. These firms place their own names on the disks and include different manuals with the DOS packages they provide. Some firms add a modified utility program or two as an improvement, but all DOS versions are similar once they are loaded into a microcomputer.

When you read about DOS in this book, you can assume that the information is generalized to cover your manufacturer's version of DOS. In special cases, differences are noted. As in Chapter 1, the terminology is simple. Again, there's nothing mystical about DOS; it is designed to simplify your relationship with your microcomputer.

Understanding DOS Files

2

The collection of programs that make up DOS is stored on a disk in a file. Files can be sorted into a variety of categories.

Text files are created by a word processing program. A text file might be a letter written to your Aunt Sadie in Podunk. Another kind of text file is the one that comes with most software. Often, the file is titled README.DOC. Usually, this file supplies instructions for the program, in case your cocker spaniel chewed up the printed booklet.

The COM file extension identifies a *command file*. A COM file is a true program that supplies your PC with instructions and information.

A disk's file name can be as long as eight digits, or as short as one. You also can add a period and a three-digit extension to the file name: SADIE.LET, for example.

What Different Files Do

Over the years, a kind of shorthand has developed to simplify identification of computer files. This identification appears as the extension at the end of the file name.

Table 2.1 shows some examples of the files that make up DOS.

Table 2.1
Examples of Files That Make Up DOS

File name	*Description*
`COMMAND.COM, FORMAT.COM, EDLIN.COM, BACKUP.COM`	The COM file extension identifies a *command* file. Command files are derived from one of the earliest operating systems for personal computers, CP/M-80. Most of the file names with COM extensions are the names of external DOS commands.

Table 2.1—(continued)

File name	Description
EGA.CPI, LCD.COM	Files with CPI extensions operate the display screen.
SELECT.DAT	A file with the extension DAT is a data file.
TYPEMAN.BAS	A program written in the BASIC language ends in BAS. Many games are written in BASIC.
AUTOEXEC.BAT	A batch file ends with the letters BAT. DOS looks for a batch file of this name and runs it automatically when you start your computer.
SHELL.CLR	CLR is a color configuration file that indicates to DOS V4.0 how to display the Shell program.
FIND.EXE, MEM.EXE, JOIN.EXE, SHELLC.EXE	Executable program files end in EXE. Aside from technical details of their internal structure, they are much like COM files. By entering the root name of an EXE file, you cause a program to run.
SELECT.HLP	HLP files display on-screen assistance.
DOSUTIL.MEU	MEU extensions indicate that the files handle on-screen menus from which you make selections.
PCMSDRV.MOS	These MOS file extensions identify files that operate a mouse.
GRAPHICS.PRO	A file that contains *profiles* of *graphics*-mode printers supported by DOS V4.0.
KEYBOARD.SYS, CONFIG.SYS, ANSI.SYS, VDISK.SYS	SYS files are system files. They are also called device drivers.

If you ask DOS for a directory listing (by typing the DIR command), the dot for the extension DOES NOT appear. DOS manuals don't explain, but certainly the roots of this curious behavior are sunk deep in the antiquity of DOS folklore.

Over the years, many "DOS handlers," or DOS shells, that appeared on the market remedied this situation. In fact, the DOS V4.0 Shell adds an extension dot to file listings. This book covers the DOS Shell in Chapter 3.

What a file listing looks like on screen:	*What file names really look like:*
COMMAND COM	COMMAND.COM
EGA CPI	EGA.CPI
SELECT DAT	SELECT.DAT
TYPEMAN BAS	TYPEMAN.BAS
AUTOEXEC BAT	AUTOEXEC.BAT
SHELL CLR	SHELL.CLR
FIND EXE	FIND.EXE
SELECT HLP	SELECT.HLP
DOSUTIL MEU	DOSUTIL.MEU
PCMSDRV MOS	PCMSDRV.MOS
GRAPHICS PRO	GRAPHICS.PRO
KEYBOARD SYS	KEYBOARD.SYS

The Three Parts of DOS

DOS can be viewed as having three main functional components:

- The command interpreter
- The file and input/output system
- The utilities

These three components are contained in files that come with your DOS package. In the following sections you are introduced to the components and to their duties.

The Command Interpreter

The Command Interpreter is DOS's "electronic butler." It interacts with you through the keyboard and screen when you operate your computer. The command interpreter is also known as the command processor and is often referred to as, simply, COMMAND.COM (command dot com).

COMMAND.COM prints DOS's requests on your display. When you enter a command, you are really telling COMMAND.COM to interpret what you have typed and to process your input so that DOS can take the appropriate action. COMMAND.COM handles the technical details of such common tasks as displaying a list of the contents of a disk, copying files, and starting programs.

The File and Input/Output System

The so-called "hidden" files are another part of the operating system. In fact, these files really are hidden, because they are classified so as not to appear in a file listing on your screen.

In time, you might want to purchase a separate "DOS handler" utility program. These software packages let you peek at files not normally shown. Many good ones exist. The more you become familiar with DOS and your PC, the more adventurous you can get. Half the fun of reading this book is learning the basics for becoming a PC sleuth. You needn't be highly technical to open up a new world to investigate.

In any event, the two or three hidden files (the number depends on your computer) define the hardware to the software. When you start a computer, these DOS system files are loaded into RAM. Combined, the files provide a unified set of routines for controlling and directing the computer's operations. These files are known as the input/output system.

The hidden files interact with special read-only memory (ROM) on the mother board. The special ROM is called the ROM Basic Input Output System, or *BIOS*. Responding to a program's request for service, the system files translate the request and pass it to the ROM BIOS. The BIOS provides a further translation of the request that links the request to the hardware.

It is largely the DOS input/output system, through the special BIOS, that determines the degree of a non-IBM PC's "IBM compatibility."

2

The Utility Files

The DOS utilities carry out useful housekeeping tasks, such as preparing disks, comparing files, finding the free space on a disk, and printing in the background. Several utilities supply statistics on disk size and memory while others compare disks and files. The utility programs are files that reside on disk and are loaded into memory by COMMAND.COM when you type their command names. These are often called *external* commands because they are not built into DOS.

By now you may suspect that DOS makes technical moves that are difficult to understand. True, much of DOS's activity falls into a technical category, but the features you need to master to make DOS work for you are easy to understand. This section briefly describes the DOS functions you will use repeatedly as your expertise grows. Later chapters treat these topics in detail.

Disk operating systems insulate you and your programs from the need to know exactly how to make the hardware work. An example is listing the contents of a disk in a disk drive. You don't need to know the capacity or recording format of the disk or how to tell the computer to direct the output to the screen; DOS does all of this for you. Another example: applications programs that store data on a disk do not have to reserve space on the disk, keep track of where on the disk the data is stored, or know how the data is encoded. DOS takes care of all these tasks.

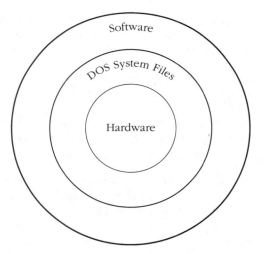

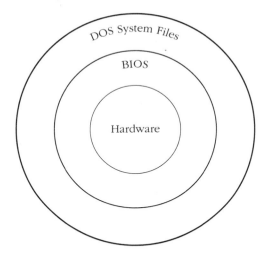

DOS provides a uniform service to the hardware by getting support from the permanent ROM BIOS in the computer. ROM BIOS can vary among computer makers, but your computer is highly compatible if the design of the ROM BIOS is integrated with DOS.

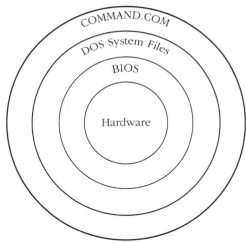

Your communications with DOS are actually instructions to COMMAND.COM. COMMAND.COM is a special type of software that lets you address the file and input/output systems of the computer through the keyboard. You instruct COMMAND.COM, rather than the hardware directly. You never need to know the details of how the hardware operates.

2

The DOS V4.0 Shell is a user-friendly program interface between your need for DOS services and the details of DOS commands. The Shell is a final layer that insulates you from learning how to control details of the computer's hardware.

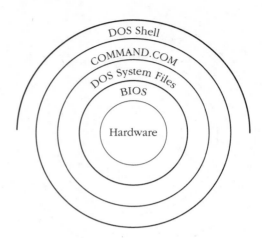

What DOS Does

DOS's many activities can be organized into several general categories. The following sections describe the most frequently performed services of DOS.

Managing Files

One of DOS's main functions is to help you organize the files that you store on your disks. Organized files are a sign of good computer housekeeping. Good housekeeping becomes crucial once you begin to take advantage of the storage capacity available on today's disks.

For example, the smallest-capacity floppy disk can hold the equivalent of 100 letter-sized pages of information. Now, imagine that each sheet of information makes up one file: you have 100 files to track! If you use disks that can hold more information than a standard floppy (such as a hard disk), file organization becomes even more crucial.

Fortunately, DOS gives you the tools to be a good computer housekeeper. DOS lists files, tells their names and sizes, and gives the dates when they were created or last modified. You can use this information for many organizational purposes. In addition to organizing files, DOS provides commands to duplicate files, discard outdated files, and replace files whose file names match.

2

Managing Disks

Certain DOS functions are essential to all computer users. For example, all disks must be prepared before they can be used in your computer. This preparation is called *formatting* and includes checking disks for available space. Other functions in DOS's disk-management category are

- Electronically labeling disks
- Making reconstructable backup copies of files for security purposes
- Restoring damaged files on disk
- Copying disks
- Viewing the contents of files on a disk

Redirecting Input and Output

DOS expects its input to come from a standard place, such as the keyboard. DOS sends its output to a standard place, such as the display screen. Designers of DOS, recognizing that it is at times convenient to send output to another device, such as a printer, provided DOS with the ability to *redirect*, or send in other directions, data that normally goes to the standard output. Through redirection, a list of files that appears on the screen can be sent to a printer or to a modem.

Running Applications Programs

Computers require complex and exact instructions, or *programs*, to provide you useful output. Computing would be totally impractical if you had to write a program for each job you needed to complete. Happily, this extra work is not necessary. Programmers spend months writing the specialized code that permits computers to function as many different tools: word processor, database manipulator, spreadsheet, and graphics generator. Through these programs, the computer's capabilities are applied to a task. These programs are called *applications programs*.

Applications programs are distributed on disks. DOS is the go-between that lets you access these programs through the computer. By simply inserting a disk into a computer's disk drive and pressing a few keys on the keyboard, you have at hand a wide variety of applications.

2

Applications programs constantly need to read data from disk files, to see what you have typed, and to send information to the screen or printer. These input and output operations are common, repetitive computer tasks. DOS furnishes applications with a simple connection, or program *interface*, that sees to the details of these repetitive activities. As you use your computer, you may want to view information about disk files, memory size, and computer configuration. DOS provides these services.

Running Batch Files

Most of your interaction with DOS takes place through the keyboard. You type commands for COMMAND.COM to carry out. These commands also can be placed in a disk file, called a *batch file*, and "played back" to COMMAND.COM. COMMAND.COM responds to these batches of commands from the file exactly as if the commands were typed from the keyboard. Batch files automate often-used command sequences, making keyboard operation simpler. Hard-to-remember command sequences make ideal candidates for batch-file treatment.

Handling Miscellaneous Tasks

Some DOS functions fall into the miscellaneous category. One example is the setting of the computer's clock and calendar so that files and applications programs can have access to dates and times. You might need to use DOS's text editor to create text files, such as memos or notes. You can even see the amount of computer memory available for application programs.

The Importance of Knowing the Uses of DOS

When you consider that your computer won't start without DOS, it should be clear that anyone using a personal computer benefits from a working knowledge of DOS. Sure, someone may be more-or-less willing to do the DOS-related work for you so that you can avoid learning about the operating system. However, if you learn DOS basics, you will become much more skilled at computing. The reward—gaining the computer's use as a productivity tool—far exceeds the effort you spend learning DOS.

In the following chapters, you will see that DOS is useful in a variety of ways. More than 70 DOS commands and functions exist. However, this book emphasizes the features needed to use a personal computer to run off-the-shelf programs. You can quickly become familiar with the essentials of DOS through this easy, step-by-step approach.

Development of DOS

Table 2.2 lists some of the important improvements and changes among the different versions of DOS, beginning in 1981.

Table 2.2
Quick Reference to Versions of DOS

MS-DOS Version	Significant Change
1.0	Original version of DOS.
1.25	Accommodates double-sided disks.
2.0	Includes multiple directories needed to organize hard disks.
3.0	Uses high-capacity floppy disks, the RAM disk, volume names, and the ATTRIB command. ATTRIB allows you to mark and unmark files, making them "read-only." This means they can't be accidentally changed or erased while being used. 3.1 includes networking.
3.2	Accommodates 3 1/2-inch drives.
3.3	Accommodates high-capacity 3 1/2-inch drives; includes new commands.
4.0	Introduces the DOS shell and the MEM command; accommodates larger files and disk capacities.

2

Experts estimate that a typical computer user spends about 20% of his time using DOS. DOS facilitates the use of applications programs.

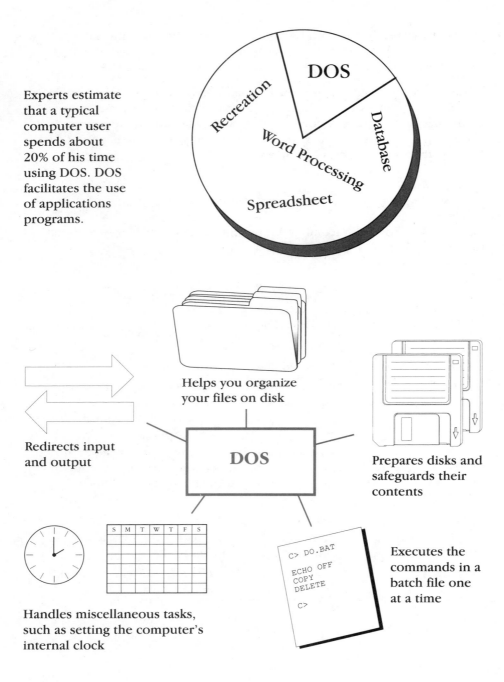

Helps you organize your files on disk

Redirects input and output

DOS

Prepares disks and safeguards their contents

Handles miscellaneous tasks, such as setting the computer's internal clock

```
C> DO.BAT
ECHO OFF
COPY
DELETE
C>
```

Executes the commands in a batch file one at a time

Lessons Learned

■ Learning DOS is a task you shouldn't fear.

■ There are basic categories of software, which can be defined by a three-letter file-name extension.

■ Files contain information stored on the magnetic surface of a disk.

■ Some files hold instructions; others contain data. Some DOS files are hidden, but all are helpful.

■ Batch files give programming potential to nonprogrammers.

■ DOS provides your computer with "behind the scenes" assistance.

■ DOS is designed to put you in full control of your PC.

■ COMMAND.COM is the most efficient assistant you've ever had.

DOS may be a loyal servant, but you will next give it the boot!

2

47

2

Giving DOS the Boot

Put on your goggles and prepare for takeoff. Don't worry; you won't fly solo. Before leaving the ground, however, you should first taxi around the runway a bit. That's what you'll do for the next few pages, as you learn the methods of operation and basic controls of your computer and DOS.

The first two chapters of this book showed you the inside of the computer, how it and DOS evolved, and how peripherals enhance your system. This chapter explains how to get your PC up and running and such related topics as setting the computer's internal clock and changing display colors. You'll find just enough definitions to keep you from being confused by DOS.

At times, you might wonder whether the time you spend learning the basics of DOS is necessary. After all, it's not as gratifying as flipping a switch or turning a key and seeing an instant physical response. Rest assured; you'll find the time well invested when you gain enough computer mastery to make intelligent decisions. When you've finished this book, no quick-talking salesperson or self-proclaimed DOS wizard will intimidate you.

You can consider your computer as a link in a technological chain. Now, you are going to bring your PC to life.

3

Key Terms Used in This Chapter

Cold boot   Flipping your PC's on/off switch to on.

Warm boot   Restarting, or resetting, a PC without turning your PC off.

Cursor   The blinking line or solid block that marks where the next keyboard entry will appear.

Default   A condition or value that the computer, the program, or DOS assumes if you choose not to supply your own conditions or values. An example is the display screen, which a computer normally uses to communicate with you.

Prompt   Symbol, character, or characters that lets you know you must enter information before anything else can happen.

DOS prompt   The characters COMMAND.COM displays to let you know you can enter a DOS command. An example is C>.

Command   A text directive to COMMAND.COM, issued at the DOS prompt, that instructs DOS to perform a task.

Parameter   A directive that adds more instructions to a command. For example, you can instruct DOS to show you the names of files on a disk. The command is DIR. To specify a certain disk, you would add the name of the drive that holds the disk (A:, for example). The drive name is a parameter.

Syntax   The proper form of commands and parameters that you type at the prompt. COMMAND.COM interprets the syntax. Communicating with a computer is much like talking with a young child. Both are limited in their vocabulary, and both take words literally.

Logged drive   The default disk drive DOS uses to carry out commands that involve disk services. Unless you change the prompt with a command, the letter of the default drive is the DOS prompt.

Definitions Made Simple

Most computer terms have simple origins and meanings. For example, to boot your PC means either turning on the computer (*cold boot*) or instructing the computer to reset itself without your turning it off (*warm boot*). The derivation comes from the expression, "pulling yourself up by your bootstraps."

Much of this chapter emphasizes DOS V4.XX, rather than earlier versions. However, there's much to be said for DOS V3.3, and many experienced users prefer this earlier release. V3.3 uses considerably less system memory than V4.XX.

Incidentally, there is no DOS V4.XX. The Xs are used here to mean any refinement of DOS V4. To date, this group includes DOS V4.00 and V4.01.

Software developers love the decimal-number concept. By definition, the smaller the decimal increment of a new version, the fewer refinements you will find. A jump to the next higher whole number implies a quantum leap in technology. The improvement is usually there, but occasionally the new number is simply a sales-boosting technique.

Many knowledgeable people feel that the Shell used in DOS V4.XX is less versatile than similar utilities you can buy separately. Because your PC probably shipped with this release of DOS, however, it deserves attention.

Don't be intimidated by the term *shell*. It's simply a program that acts as an interface between you and DOS. Often, shells make using your PC easier, and many experienced PC owners use them. On the other hand, like automatic cameras, DOS shells can make a beginner somewhat lazy and, worse, might keep you from learning important DOS basics.

Advanced photographers understand the fundamentals of their art. This allows them to use their skill and creativity with today's auto-everything cameras. Professional photographers combine the ease of use of the latest generation of auto-focus, motor-drive cameras with optics theory, photographic skills, and artistic composition. The same kind of basic knowledge also applies to making the most of a DOS shell.

If you learn a few computer terms and the basic start-up process before you press the On button, you will feel more confident. Just remember, don't get

51

3

nervous about operations mentioned here. More than likely, you'll find the solutions with further reading, or by glancing at help screens.

With early computers, operators started by entering a binary program and instructing the computer to run the program. This binary program is called a "bootstrap loader." The term *booting* stuck; even now, booting still refers to start-up procedure. With today's DOS, the booting process is easy.

In this chapter, it is assumed that you neither know how to boot your computer nor know the process that occurs during booting. Actually, booting is as simple as turning on your stereo. Right now, you probably feel more uncomfortable powering up a PC, but this situation will change.

Creating a Good Physical Environment

Before leaving the ground, a pilot runs through a checklist to affirm that the aircraft is airworthy. As a pilot's preliminary check is important, so too is a check of your computer equipment. Preliminary checks prevent later crashes.

Computers like clean, steady current. Choose a good electrical outlet that does not serve devices like copy machines, hair dryers, or other electrical gadgets. Ask your computer dealer about a line conditioner if you must share an outlet. Make sure that the switch is off before you plug in your computer. Some computers have switches marked with 0 and 1. The position marked 0 is off.

Your PC needs room to breathe. Computers must dissipate the heat generated by the electronic components. Keep paper, books, beverages, and other clutter away from the system unit's case. More important, make sure that the cooling fan in back of your PC works properly. Electronic components and excessive heat do not mix well. This is particularly true in humid environments.

Have your DOS manual, DOS disks, and PC system documentation nearby for reference. Even if you don't use the manuals often, they make good paperweights.

Following good work habits in an unfamiliar environment can save you a lot of grief. It's comparable to stressing that new drivers wear seat belts, although belts may initially feel uncomfortable.

Booting Your PC

The disk that boots your computer might be labeled "Startup," "System," "Main," or "DOS." Check your manual if you are uncertain which disk is bootable or ask your computer specialist for a bootable DOS system disk. From here on, the bootable DOS disk is called the DOS Master disk.

The Cold Boot

The cold boot consists of two steps: inserting the floppy disk in drive A and turning the computer's switch on.

Note that if your computer supplier installed DOS on your hard disk, you can automatically boot from the hard disk by simply turning on the computer. To understand the elements of booting, however, you should learn to boot from a floppy disk.

Insert the DOS Master disk into drive A. Check your PC's system manual for the location of drive A and for disk-insertion instructions. Depending on your system unit's configuration, drive A is the left slot (for vertically positioned drives) or top slot (for horizontally positioned drives) in the system unit's cabinet. A properly inserted disk usually has its label facing to the left on vertical drives and up on horizontal units.

You insert disks into horizontal and vertical drives in the same way. To complete the insertion of a 5 1/4-inch disk, close the drive door or turn the latch clockwise.

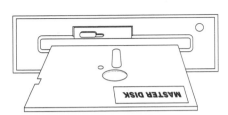
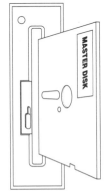

Insert 3 1/2-inch disks gently, pushing until you hear a click. The drive closes by itself.

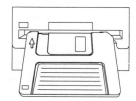

3

If the disk does not go in, make sure that the drive doesn't already hold another disk. Never force a disk into the drive door, because you could damage the disk, the drive, or both.

After inserting the disk, close the drive door (microfloppy drives close themselves). If you have a lock on the front of the system unit, unlock the unit.

Turn on the display switch, if necessary. Some displays are powered from the system unit and do not have a switch. Locate the computer's power switch, usually on the right side toward the rear of the system unit. Turn on the switch. At this point, the cold boot begins.

What Booting Looks Like

The instant you flip the switch, the computer performs a Power On Reset (POR). The RAM, the microprocessor, and other electronics are zeroed out, like a chalkboard cleaned with an eraser.

The system then begins a Power-On Self-Test (POST). POST ensures that your PC's electronics are working properly. The POST takes from a few seconds to several minutes to complete. During POST, you may see a description of the test or a blinking cursor on the display. When the POST ends, the computer beeps and drive A spins. Finally, a bootstrap loader loads DOS from the Master DOS disk into RAM.

Some computers let you watch the action of the power-on self-test (POST). The test verifies that the computer is working properly.

When DOS completes loading, the DOS prompt, or command prompt, appears. The DOS prompt is a letter and the "greater-than" (>) symbol representing the current, or active, drive.

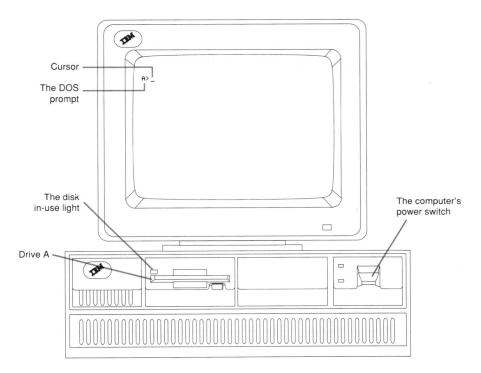

Cursor

The DOS prompt

The disk in-use light

The computer's power switch

Drive A

Looking at the DOS Shell

With DOS V4.XX, you have two view options:

- The prompt view
- The DOS Shell view

The *prompt* view is the traditional, simple look of DOS. The prompt view appears on a plain screen with one letter of the alphabet representing the current, or active, drive. The letter is followed by a "greater than" symbol. If you boot your system with the DOS disk in drive A, you see A> on the

3

screen. If your computer has a hard disk drive on which DOS is already installed, the C> appears following the boot.

Why is the letter B missing? Unless otherwise specified by the person who configured your hard drive, C> is the standard default designation. Many PCs come with only one floppy disk drive, and its default value is always A>. However, hard drive systems with two floppy drives are more convenient. Many people purchase the latter drive configuration. In such cases, the second floppy drive is designated drive B.

The Shell view is a new look for DOS, but it's been around for a long time in other forms. Over the past several years, software companies have developed and marketed inexpensive DOS shells, some of which have more features than DOS V4.XX's Shell.

The Shell view provides a full-screen window with various menus, pop-up help boxes, and graphic presentation of directories and files. You can issue some standard DOS commands by using a mouse to point to and select pull-down menus and dialog boxes.

By the way, a mouse is almost a prerequisite for many shells, desktop publishing programs, and the latest generation of "windows-style" software. If, on the other hand, you know your way around a typewriter keyboard, you can perform some functions more quickly in the DOS Shell with cursor keys.

The Shell view is the friendliest way to use DOS, but it can be a wolf in sheep's clothing. You should understand the basic commands before relying on the Shell. Also, typing a command gives the user time to reflect upon the act. Although you will use only a few DOS commands with frequency, the need to know them becomes clear as you gain experience.

When using the Shell, you must learn not only the Shell's features, you should also know the DOS commands that these features represent. Another complicating factor is that some Shell commands might be different on various compatible computers. For the most part, the generic DOS prompt view remains essentially the same on every DOS computer.

For many users the Shell feels easier to master than DOS, but you can still profit from knowing the DOS commands and terminology. V4.XX commands remain substantially unchanged from previous versions of DOS. The Shell is a shortcut for those who already understand the basics of DOS.

The First Look at the DOS Shell

DOS's new look began with version 4.0. The Shell view is a full-screen window with menus and pop-up help screens.

If you have DOS V4.XX, read this section. We'll detail V4.XX installation later, in an appendix. For what it's worth, setting up either DOS V3.3 or V4.XX is not difficult. Questions are asked and replies are required. This is particularly true in any DOS version before V4.XX.

The Shell provides a visual presentation of DOS with "action options" from which you make selections. You can manage your computer from the action options, which are function- and cursor- key selectable versions of the DOS prompt-view commands. The following sections highlight the basic structure of the Shell.

The prompt view in versions of DOS before V4.0 displays only the system prompt. Common DOS prompts are A> and C> for floppy and hard drives, respectively. The first screen in DOS V4.XX, Start Programs, lists the main items in the Shell. You can add your applications to this list.

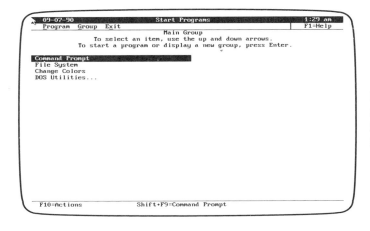

DOS V4.XX presents a new user interface, the DOS Shell.

The DOSSHELL Command

If the Shell is not already loaded, type **DOSSHELL** at the DOS prompt and then press Enter to load the DOS Shell into memory. DOS establishes the Shell's system configuration that was chosen when DOS V4.XX was installed.

57

(A batch file holds the configuration commands for the DOS Shell.) For now, assume that the options selected are valid for your computer.

The DOS Shell loads a few seconds after you enter the DOSSHELL command from the DOS prompt. If your system goes directly to the Shell when you boot your computer, it isn't necessary to type the DOSSHELL command.

3

`Start Programs` is the first screen you see in the Shell. The Start Programs screen serves as your base for exploring the important keystrokes you'll use while in the DOS Shell. On either side of the screen title, the time and date appear. Below the title is the action bar, a line that displays the actions you can select. Positioned under the action bar, you'll find the group title line and the group contents.

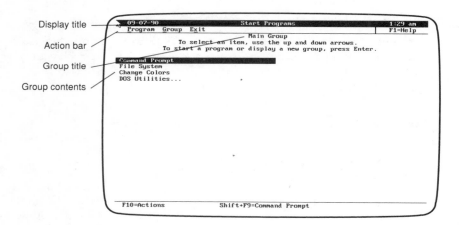

On-line Help

Fortunately, you can always call up information about DOS when you use the Shell. This ability is not unique to the DOS Shell. User-friendly help screens are part of virtually all top-of-the-line shell software. When you press F1, a help window appears. On-line help assists you with the current selection or action to help you make an informed selection.

⌐F1⌐ Displays a help window on screen.

Pressing F1 and then F11 displays a directory of different help topics. If your computer lacks an F11 key, use the Alt-F1 combination. Within the help window, you can press F9 to display a list of the keys and their Shell

58

meanings. Within a window, you can scroll up or down a window of text with PgUp or PgDn. The Shell sounds a beep when you press keys that don't have a function. Press Esc to cancel the help window and resume your session.

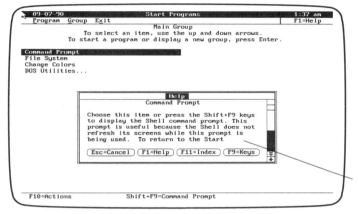

DOS V4.XX includes an on-line help feature. This screen shows the Command Prompt item highlighted.

Help screen

Moving from Shell to Prompt

You can go from the Shell to the DOS prompt and still keep the Shell in memory. To do so, use the cursor-arrow keys to place the highlight bar on Command Prompt and press Enter. (The bar, also called the *selection cursor*, is a highlighted, reversed video, or different-color section of text. The highlight bar is used to select an object for an action when you press Enter or click the mouse button.)

When you press Enter, the DOS prompt appears. You now can type DOS commands. To return to the Shell, type **Exit** and press Enter. For convenience, you can also press Shift-F9 to get to the command prompt. By selecting Command Prompt from the group items, however, you can see how the selection process works.

If you cannot move your selection cursor, check to make sure that Num Lock is off and that the actions on the action bar are highlighted, or reversed, from the surrounding display. Use the right- and left-arrow keys to move the highlight accordingly. F10 moves the activity area of the selection cursor between actions and items. Press F10 until no action item stands out from the rest.

The other way to get to the DOS command prompt is to leave the Shell. This method erases the Shell from memory. To stop the Shell, press F10 and place the selection cursor on Exit. Now press Enter. Move the selection cursor to Exit Shell, if necessary, and press Enter. The Shell returns you to the DOS prompt. Because you have exited the Shell, you must restart the Shell by typing **DOSSHELL** when you want to use it again.

Navigating in the Shell

Now that you know how to get to the DOS command prompt from within the Shell, you can look at the other Main Group items. The Main Group of the opening Start Programs screen shows the major areas where you work in the Shell. By selecting one of these items, you are asking the Shell to usher you to a screen so that you can work in that item's subject area. The following exercises demonstrate moving around DOS Shell screens.

The Start Programs Screen

The Start Programs screen offers a Main Group of Shell items. Certain items are already set up in DOS V4.XX. These are Command Prompt, File System, Change Colors, and DOS Utilities. Users who are familiar with DOS can add their own. Some software makers offer installation procedures for their programs that add their programs to the item list. Here's how you move around the Start Program Screen:

1. To move to the selection cursor to the action bar, press F10.

   The action bar gives you options for how the Shell presents the activity in the window below the action bar. You do DOS work in the lower part of the screen and give the Shell instructions with the action bar. You can, for example, add or change a program or a group of programs or delete items from the group. The Shell knows which items in a selection list aren't usable at that point and puts an asterisk in the item's name. If you have an EGA or VGA display, the Shell makes the names of unavailable items look "fuzzy," rather than using the asterisk.

2. Press Enter to select an action item. Additional selections pull down from under the selected item automatically. As with other items in the Shell, selected pull-down commands are not carried out unless you press Enter.

3. Move to other items in pull-down menus, using the up- and down-arrow keys.

⟨←⟩, ⟨→⟩,   Moves the selection cursor within a section of the
⟨↑⟩, ⟨↓⟩   screen, or selects items in pull-down menus.

4. Exit pull-down menus by pressing Esc.

5. The F10 key toggles the selection cursor between the action bar and the lower work area of any Shell screen. Press F10 a few times and watch the selection cursor move to and from the action bar.

   If you have a mouse, you can move the pointer freely across area boundaries on the screen. One click selects an item. Two quick clicks select an item and tell the Shell to execute that item.

⟨F10⟩   Moves the selection cursor between the action bar and the lower part of the screen.

⟨Tab⟩   Moves the selection cursor from section to section on the screen. If you press Tab several times, the Shell selects the action bar.

Shift-F9 moves you to the command prompt, but leaves the Shell in memory.

The File System Screen

The second item listed on the Start Programs screen is File System. Use the arrow keys to select File System; then press Enter. Because DOS is a disk operating system and because disks store information in files, the Shell pays ample attention to the file system in this screen.

To move the File System screen, place the highlight on File System and press Enter.

The general layout of the File System screen resembles the layout of the Start Programs screen.

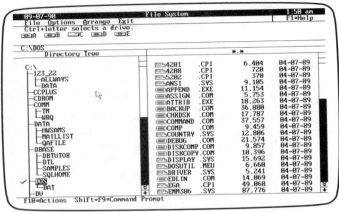

You see an action bar toward the top of the screen. Notice that the action items aren't the same as on the Start Programs screen.

Below the action bar, the remainder of the screen is divided into sections bounded by bars or included in colored blocks.

Look at the screen until you clearly see the individual sections. If you're familiar with DOS's hierarchical file structure, you'll see the screen's logic. Chapter 6 answers questions you have about directories.

The File System screen appears when you select File System from Start Programs and press ⏎Enter. The following steps will guide you through the routine.

To change the logged disk drive, press the left- and right-arrow keys. To move between screen sections, press Tab. Highlight items within sections by pressing the cursor keys.

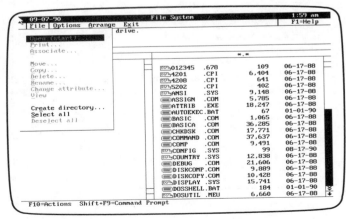

To display the File System pull-down menus, select an item from the action bar with F10. Press Enter.

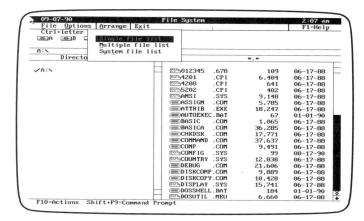

Pressing the left- and right-arrow keys displays menus for other file-system options.

3

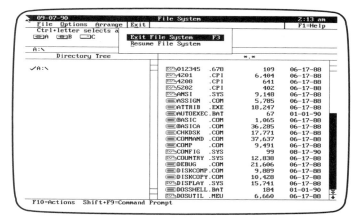

Pressing F10 or Tab returns you to the action bar from which you can select another item or exit to Start Programs.

For now, you can concentrate on learning to move around the File System screen. The following series is a practice exercise.

1. Press the F10 key a few times. You see that the selection cursor toggles between the action bar and one of the lower items. F10 works the same here as in Start Programs.

2. Press F10 until a lower item is selected.

3. Press the Tab key. The selection cursor moves to an item in the next area of the lower part of the screen. Press the Tab key a few more times. The selection cursor moves from section to section. Use the Tab key to move to the next screen section. If you press

Tab enough times, the Shell selects the action bar. You can tab so quickly that you may find that using the Tab key is more convenient for reaching the action bar than using F10.

4. Tab to the list of file names on the right side of the screen.

5. Press the down-arrow key to make the selection cursor move to the next name. Use the up- and down-arrow keys to move to items that are listed vertically; use the right- and left-arrow keys on items listed horizontally. A beep tells you when you have reached the end of the list.

6. Press F10 again to move to the action bar. Press Enter to pull down additional information items about the selection. Use the left- and right-arrow keys to move to other main action bar items.

Notice that the pulled-down list from the first selection allows the other items' pull-downs to appear automatically. You have all the selection possibilities available for viewing when you use the right- or left-arrow key. The File pull-down gives you actions for the Shell to perform on files and directories that you have selected from the lower part of the screen. The Options and Arrange pull-downs control the way the Shell shows the files or prompts you for confirmation when you erase or rename files.

Change Colors

As the next series illustrates, the DOS Shell colors are easily modified on microcomputers equipped with a graphics display adapter card.

1. Select Change Colors from the Start Programs screen and press Enter. You are now in the Change Colors utility. The Shell allows you to pick from available color schemes to give the Shell the look you prefer.

   If you have a text-only display, the Shell knows that you can't change colors, so it won't let you try this item. If you have a graphics adapter and a black and white, green, or amber screen, you'll see the colors as shades. Press the right- or left-arrow key, and your screen takes on a different look each time.

2. F1 gives you help, if you need it.

3. Look at all the combinations and stop on your favorite. Press Enter to keep that combination and then press Esc to return to the Start Programs screen.

The DOS Utilities Screen

The DOS Utilities screen is the last item on the Start Programs screen. The selections in this group are disk utilities that let you set the date and time, copy and compare files, and format, back up, and restore disks. In later chapters, you'll learn how to perform these activities from the DOS prompt. For now, try setting the date and time by following these steps:

1. Using the arrow keys, select DOS Utilities and press Enter. You are now in the DOS Utilities screen, but you're just passing through.

2. Using the arrow keys, select Set Date and Time and press Enter. A new block of the screen called a *window* pops up. This is a Shell pop-up window, and in this case, it is the Set Date and Time utility.

3. In the Set Date and Time window, you see a prompt for a new date and an example of what format the Shell expects.

4. Press F1 for an explanation of the format; then enter the date and at the cursor press Enter. Now you are prompted for the correct time.

5. Enter the time at the cursor in 24-hour format and press Enter. The Shell tells you to press any key, so press the space bar. The Shell brings you back to the DOS Utilities screen.

6. Press Esc to get back to Start Programs, F10 to move to the action bar, or Shift-F9 to go to the command prompt.

7. When you finish entering the date and time, press Esc to return to the Start Programs screen.

You have successfully navigated the DOS Shell!

Prompting and Stopping

If you entered the date and time from the Shell, you've seen how it takes you to the command line where you are prompted to enter information.

Assume that you are working from the command prompt, because you either do not use the DOS Shell or because you used the Shell to reach the command prompt. The following tasks are miscellaneous items: how to perform a warm boot, how to set the date and time from the command prompt, and why you should know about the logged disk drive. After reading this section, you'll be ready to take control of your computer with DOS.

The Warm Boot

The warm boot differs little from the cold boot. For the cold boot, you inserted the DOS system disk and then switched on the computer. For the warm boot, your PC is already running. Make sure that your DOS system disk is in drive A, or that the operating system is installed on hard disk drive C. You then press three keys.

Look at the keyboard and locate the Ctrl, Alt, and Del keys. The warm boot requires pressing and holding down Ctrl and Alt and then pressing Del. The PC skips the preliminary tests and immediately loads DOS. Don't worry if nothing happens on the first try. With some systems that have run programs, you may have to use Ctrl-Alt-Del twice.

The DATE and TIME Commands from the DOS Prompt

Most contemporary computers come with a built-in, battery-powered calendar and clock. The correct date and time are the default values. A default value is a suggested response or recommended choice or action. If you make no specific choice when the computer prompts you, DOS accepts the built-in suggestion by default. You usually press Enter to accept the default condition.

You press Enter to activate the command you have typed. Enter is like a "Go" key that instructs DOS to execute a command. When a computer boots, it automatically enters the time and date from the system, offers default values, or requires you to enter each manually.

If your computer is set up to record automatically the date and time, you do nothing during the boot process. Otherwise, DOS prompts you to enter the correct date and time.

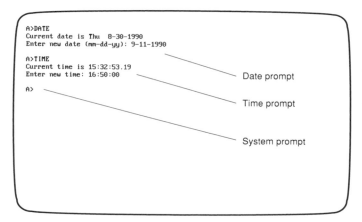

```
A>DATE
Current date is Thu  8-30-1990
Enter new date (mm-dd-yy): 9-11-1990

A>TIME
Current time is 15:32:53.19
Enter new time: 16:50:00

A>
```

Date prompt

Time prompt

System prompt

You can enter DOS commands when the command prompt appears. The boot is complete.

The Logged Drive

If you want to change the current, or *logged*, drive in DOS, type **C:** at the A> prompt. Before you press Enter, your prompt looks like this:

```
A>C:
```

After pressing the Enter key, the following appears:

```
C>_
```

Enter the drive letter followed by a colon, and don't forget to press the Enter key. DOS reads the drive letter and colon as the disk drive's name.

Once the boot is complete, the command prompt indicates the logged drive. The logged drive is the *active* drive, or the drive responding to commands.

For example, an A> with a blinking cursor tells you DOS is logged onto drive A, usually a floppy disk drive. The C> with a blinking cursor means DOS is logged onto drive C, normally a hard disk drive. You can change the logged drive from A to C by typing **C:** at the prompt and pressing Enter. Remember to type the letter C and a colon (:).

67

3

What does this mean? It means that you have instructed your PC that you want to work with any information accessible through drive C. It also means that you have begun to take charge!

DOS remembers the logged drive as its current drive. Many commands use the current drive and other current information without having to specify them in the command. You'll learn about this phenomenon later as the *rule of currents*.

Remember that you need not specify the drive if you request information from the logged drive. (Note: If you use two floppy drives and don't have a hard drive, substitute B: for C: in the examples and exercises.) You'll learn later how to include the drive name when you request information from a drive other than the current drive.

Stopping the Computer

Occasionally, you will want to stop the computer from carrying out a command. Besides switching the power off (the last resort), there are three ways to stop a command in DOS:

Ctrl Break	The Ctrl-Break combination is located next to the Reset key on some keyboards. Make sure that you do not press the Reset key when you perform a Ctrl-Break. As in all Ctrl-key sequences, you hold down the Ctrl key and then press the other key(s) in the sequence. If you frequently press the wrong keys, try using Ctrl-C.
Ctrl C	Stops commands in which DOS pauses for you to type further information. Be aware that DOS carries out many commands too quickly for you to intervene with Ctrl-C.
Ctrl Alt Del	The warm boot key sequence. Ctrl-Alt-Del should not be your first choice for stopping a command, but sometimes Ctrl-C or Ctrl-Break doesn't work. If the Ctrl-Alt-Del approach fails, turning off the power is the last resort. Some newer computers, however, come with a Reset switch that performs the same function as Ctrl-Alt-Del.

Imagine these key sequences as "panic buttons" to stop DOS. Don't worry if you have to use them to prevent disasters. Practice them with a nondestructive command, such as DIR (which is explained in the next chapter). You may perspire a little, but soon you will have everything well in hand.

Lessons Learned

■ Computer terminology is basic and simple to understand.

■ Don't be intimidated by the numbers and decimals often added to software names. These numbers identify different versions of products. The higher the number, the newer the version or release.

■ Placing XX's at the end of a product version number is computer shorthand for indicating that your statements work for all versions.

■ The booting process is automatic if the DOS system files are on a disk in the computer.

■ Providing a good environment for your computer and its software may prevent hardware failure and data loss.

■ DOS V4.XX comes with a Shell, which provides an easy way for beginners to execute DOS commands. Navigating the Shell is simple and pull-down menus list all options.

■ Changing the drive you want to use is as easy as typing a letter and colon.

Now firmly at the helm, you are ready to command DOS.

3

Using DOS commands

4

Have you ever met someone who intimidated you? Maybe the person was taller, spoke in an authoritative voice, or projected an unusually strong image. This feeling happens to everyone. Often, though, initial impressions have little to do with the true nature of a person. The same is true of DOS. Despite what you may hear, DOS is designed to be well mannered.

This chapter is in many ways the meat of the book. Here, you'll be served only prime cuts of information in a balanced diet. Shortly, you'll feel more relaxed about using your computer as you master the command-line techniques of DOS. This chapter illuminates such subjects as issuing a DOS command, understanding how commands work, using the DIR command, and wielding wild-card characters.

Getting acquainted with command syntax

Issuing commands

Adding parameters

Understanding wild cards

Using the DIR command

Understanding the directory listing

4

Key Terms Used in this Chapter

Command   A collection of characters that tells the computer what you want it to do. Most commands are contractions of English words, with single numbers or letters often added as optional instructions.

Syntax   The specific set of rules you follow when you issue commands.

Parameter   An additional instruction in the command syntax that refines what you want the DOS command to do.

Switch   A part of the command that turns on an optional instruction or function.

Delimiter   A character that separates the parts of a command. Common delimiters are the space and the slash.

Wild card   A character you substitute for another (or more than one) character.

Important Concepts about Commands

To tell DOS what you want it to do, you enter DOS *commands*. Commands are letters, numbers, and acronyms, separated—or *delimited*—by certain other characters. Stripped of jargon, DOS command usage is like telling your dog to "sit," "heel," and "stay." Additionally, you can tell your computer to "sit and bark" concurrently. DOS commands frequently, though not exclusively, use slash marks (/) to represent such additional instructions.

A command you give to DOS is similar to a written instruction you might give to a work associate, but with DOS you must be precise. People use interconnecting words and inferences that the human brain can easily grasp. DOS knows only what its developers programmed it to understand.

When you type a command in its proper form—or *syntax*—at the DOS prompt, both the DOS command and any additional instructions communicate your intent. Both relay the action you want to perform and the object of that action. Remember, your main tool for communication with your PC is the keyboard. Your PC is ready to work for you, but it doesn't respond to humor, anger, frustration, or imprecise syntax.

Assume that you have an assistant with a limited vocabulary. If you want a sign on a bulletin board duplicated for posting on another bulletin board, you might instruct, "Copy sign A to sign B. Make sure that the copy is free from errors."

Similarly, if you want DOS to duplicate the data disk in drive A on a disk you've placed in drive B, you would give DOS the following instruction:

DISKCOPY A: B:

To have DOS, the efficient helper, compare the copy and the original, type this:

DISKCOMP A: B:

DISKCOPY and DISKCOMP are good examples of DOS commands that are clearly named to explain the activity they execute. The letters A: and B: are the disk drives you want DOS to use.

Although you'll rarely use more than 10 commands, DOS recognizes and responds to more than 50 commands. The most common of these commands are built into the command processor (COMMAND.COM) and are instantly available at the system prompt. Because these commands are always ready for use, they are called *internal* commands.

Other commands are stored as individual programs on your DOS disk. If your PC has a hard drive, these programs have more than likely been placed on drive C in a special subdivision. In the public library, such a subdivision might be called a "section of specialty." On a hard disk or on a floppy disk, it is called a *directory*.

These commands are located, loaded, and executed when you type them at the system prompt and press Enter. They are called *external* commands. External commands can execute from the system prompt in the same way as internal commands. Chapter 6 details using both types of commands.

Learning the ins and outs of issuing DOS commands takes practice. DOS commands follow a logical structure, but that structure is rigid.

The strength of DOS is that once you understand its rules, everything flows easily. Commands conform to standard rules in their command-line structure. DOS is easier to use when you understand the concepts behind the commands. You can then generalize rules to different commands.

To feel comfortable with DOS commands, remember that

- DOS requires that you use a specific set of rules, or syntax, when you issue commands.
- Parameters, part of a command's syntax, can change the way a command is executed.

4

You can think of the command name as the action part of a DOS command. In addition to the name, many commands either require or allow further directions. Any such additions are called *parameters*. Parameters tell DOS what to apply the action to or how to apply the action. Using DOS commands is quite easy if you follow the rules of order and use the correct parameters.

The worst part about many DOS manuals is that they present you with something that may resemble a French menu if you speak no French. And, like the waiter standing over you with a casually smug attitude, these other DOS books make little effort to help you navigate through the menu.

In fact, most DOS manuals are agony for the novice. Even the experienced user can be driven to hair pulling in fruitless quests for information.

MS-DOS QuickStart, 2nd Edition, is designed to be pleasurably read from cover to cover. It introduces DOS to new users, but much of it can serve as a review for the more experienced user. This book makes a gourmet presentation, but the menu is in English.

Syntax

Syntax is the structure, order, and vocabulary in which you type the elements of the DOS command. Using proper syntax when you enter a DOS command is comparable to using proper English when you speak. DOS must clearly understand what you are typing to carry out the command.

Unfortunately, many DOS manuals use "symbolic form" to describe command syntax, without revealing what each term means. Such books frequently list every command switch (option), as though multiple switches were a normal part of the command.

In fact, many DOS commands cannot be issued to accept every possible option. Using all the options is like ordering a sandwich with white, rye, whole wheat *and* cinnamon-raisin bread. The choice is usually either/or, rather than all. A command should contain nothing more than what you want to instruct DOS to do.

Simply stated, symbolic form is the use of a letter or name for illustrative purposes. A file used to illustrate a command might be called EXAMPLE.COM. Actually, EXAMPLE.COM exists only in the mind of the writer. It is an example. When you enter the real command, you are supposed to substitute a real name for the symbolic one.

Symbolic form is used to describe not only files, but also the entire command line. A DIR command shown in symbolic form looks like this:

> **DIR *d:filename.ext*/W/P**

This command can be defined as follows:

> **DIR *d: (drive:) filename.ext* /W/P *(switches)***

For example, a command you might use in the real world looks like this:

> **DIR C:/P**

As you can see, symbolic notation can confuse, rather than enlighten, until you understand the concept behind the form.

Switches

A *switch* is a parameter that turns on an optional function of a command. In the DIR example, /W and /P are switches. Note that each switch is a character preceded by a slash. Not all DOS commands use switches. In addition, switches may have different meanings for different commands.

You can use the /W switch with the DIR command to display a wide directory of files. Normally, DIR displays a directory with one file listing per line. The date and time the file was created is displayed next to the file name. As the screen fills, the first files scroll off the top of the display. The /W switch displays a directory listing that shows only file names and extensions.

Sometimes a disk contains too many files to display on one screen. When you use the /P switch with the directory command, 23 lines of files, or approximately one screen full, are displayed. The display pauses when the screen fills. At the bottom of a paused directory, DOS prompts you to Press any key to continue to move to the next screen full of files. The /P switch thus allows you to see all the files in the directory, one screen at a time.

When DOS says Press any key to continue, it means to press *almost* any key. If you press the Shift, Alt, Caps Lock, Num Lock, or Scroll Lock keys, DOS ignores you. The easiest keys to press are the space bar or the Enter key.

Many DOS commands can be typed in several forms and still be correct. Although the simple versions of DOS syntax work effectively, most DOS manuals show the complete syntax for a command, which again can confuse you. For example, the syntax for the DIR command looks like this:

Now, break down the sample command piece by piece. You'll see that, rather than being an actual command, it is the symbolic form of all the alternatives.

DIR	You want a directory listing to be run. A normal directory listing without any switches (options) appears in vertical form. The listing shows not only file names, but also the file size and the time and date of each file's last modification. To get this listing, type **DIR**. Do not leave a space between the > symbol and the name.
d:	The drive containing the directory listing. If the system prompt indicates the drive you want, you don't need to write anything. If you want a directory listing of another drive, type the appropriate drive letter.

76

filename.ext   Symbolic form meaning "substitute the file name." DOS never allows more than one file with the same name in any one directory. Other than to display that one file's size and the amount of space free on that disk, the term has little meaning when you use the DIR command.

For example, the following command adds the file-name parameter:

DIR C:MYFILE.TXT

In symbolic notation, MYFILE.TXT is shown as *filename.ext*.

/W   A switch for the DIR command. /W requests that DOS display a horizontal (or wide) directory listing, instead of showing a single vertical listing. The wide listing provides no information other than the file name. The command DIR/W displays a wide directory listing. The / is the delimiter. It tells DOS that a switch is about to follow.

/P   Normally, DOS scrolls down a directory from beginning to end without stopping. The /P switch requests a pause when the screen is filled. Pressing a key lists another screen of files.

Typing DIR at the DOS prompt produces a directory of the disk that is on the logged drive. Long listings may scroll off the screen.

To halt scrolling temporarily, press Ctrl S or Pause

Press any key to continue. On enhanced keyboards, you also can press Pause

You might type the DIR command in any of the following ways:

C>DIR
C>DIR/P
C>DIR/W
C>DIR/W/P
C>DIR A:
C>DIR A:/P

```
DOS          <DIR>      09-11-90    9:41p
FASTBACK     <DIR>      09-11-90    9:50p
FIGURES      <DIR>      09-11-90   10:00p
GAMES        <DIR>      09-11-90   10:01p
HG           <DIR>      09-11-90   10:26p
INSET        <DIR>      09-11-90   10:55p
JEOPARDY     <DIR>      09-11-90   10:01p
MOUSE        <DIR>      09-11-90   10:01p
NU           <DIR>      09-11-90   10:01p
PBRUSH       <DIR>      09-11-90   10:27p
PM           <DIR>      09-11-90   10:28p
PROGEN       <DIR>      09-11-90   10:29p
TOOLBOOK     <DIR>      09-11-90   10:29p
TP           <DIR>      09-11-90   10:02p
WINDOWS3     <DIR>      09-11-90   10:30p
WORD5        <DIR>      09-11-90   10:03p
WORDSTAR     <DIR>      09-11-90   10:06p
AUTOEXEC BAT          166 09-11-90 10:39p
Press any key to continue . . .

COMMAND  COM      37557 04-07-89   12:00a
CONFIG   SYS        157 09-11-90   10:13p
         25 File(s)   10674176 bytes free

C:\>
```

The command DIR/P displays the directory listing page by page. The command itself scrolls off the screen when you press a key to continue listing the directory.

```
C:\>DIR /W

 Volume in drive C is DOS400
 Volume Serial Number is 266E-1CEF
 Directory of  C:\

123          CAKEWALK     CCPLUS       COMM         CONFIGS
DOS          FASTBACK     FIGURES      GAMES        HG
INSET        JEOPARDY     MOUSE        NU           PBRUSH
PM           PROGEN       TOOLBOOK     TP           WINDOWS3
WORD5        WORDSTAR     AUTOEXEC BAT COMMAND  COM CONFIG   SYS
         25 File(s)   10674176 bytes free

C:\>
```

The command DIR/W displays the directory listing in a wide arrangement, but you lose information about individual files.

Don't worry about your PC pulling something sneaky when you type a command. No command you type is executed until you press the Enter key. Operating DOS is simpler than you might expect. Just remember that as you gain experience you may begin to use even potentially dangerous commands in a routine manner.

To show you how routine DOS commands can be potentially dangerous, consider one that strikes fear in every new PC user: the *DEL*, or *ERASE*, command.

78

Experienced computer users make mistakes with DEL more than with any other DOS command. They occasionally zip through their work in a careless manner. In most instances, DOS is forgiving. After all, who really cares if you accidentally type a request to view a directory of a different drive than you really want? Retyping the instruction properly is a simple matter. The DEL command, however, is an exception.

The DEL and the ERASE commands are one and the same. They are your way of asking that a file or group of files be erased from a designated directory. If you allow yourself to get careless when issuing this command, you can get into big trouble. More information on the DEL command appears in Chapter 7.

Issuing Commands

The command name is a key to DOS. The command processor COMMAND.COM reads the command you type. COMMAND.COM can carry out several "built-in" commands. It also knows how to load and run the external utility programs you enter at the DOS prompt.

Typing the Command Name

When you type a command, do not leave a space after the greater-than sign (>) of the DOS prompt. Enter the DOS command name directly after the prompt. If the command has no parameters or switches, press the Enter key after the last letter of the command name. For example, you type the directory command as **DIR** at the prompt and then press Enter.

Adding Parameters

When you are to enter parameters that are not switches, this book shows them in two ways: lower- and uppercase. You must supply the value for the lowercase text. The lowercase letters are shorthand for the full names of the parts of a command. Uppercase means that you enter letter-for-letter what you see.

Remember that you delimit, or separate, parameters from the rest of the command. Most of the time the delimiter is a space, but other delimiters, such as the comma (,), the backslash (\), and the colon (:) exist. Just look at the examples in this book to learn the correct delimiter.

If the example command has switches, you can recognize them by the preceding slash (/). Always enter the switch letter as shown. Remember to type the slash.

Ignoring a Command Line (Esc)

4

You'll make mistakes when entering commands. Until you press the Enter key, fortunately, DOS does not act on the command. You can correct a mistake by using the arrow keys or the Backspace key to reposition the cursor. Press the Esc key if you want to start again from the beginning. The Esc key withdraws the entry and gives you a new line. Just remember that these line-editing and canceling tips work only before you press the Enter key. Some commands can be successfully stopped with the Ctrl-C or Ctrl-Break sequence, but checking that the command is typed correctly is always good practice.

To reposition the cursor, use the arrow keys or the Backspace key. To clear the last entry, press Esc and retype the command.

```
A:\ >DIR C:MYF-\

  Volume in drive C has no label
  Volume Serial Number is E417-17EB
Invalid directory

A:\ >
```

Executing a Command

The Enter key is the action key for DOS commands. Make it a habit to pause and read what you have typed before you press Enter. After pressing Enter, the computer carries out your command. During the processing of the command, DOS does not display any keystrokes you might type. DOS does remember your keystrokes, however, so be aware that the characters you type could end up in your next command.

Using DOS Editing Keys

When you type a command line and press the Enter key, DOS copies the line into an input buffer, a storage area for commands. You can pull the last command line from the buffer and use the line again. This feature is helpful when you want to issue a command that is similar to the last command you used. Table 4.1 lists the keys you use to edit the input buffer.

Table 4.1
DOS Command Line Editing Keys

Key	Action
←, →	Moves cursor to the next tab stop.
Esc	Cancels the current line and does not change the buffer.
Ins	Enables you to insert characters in the line.
Del	Deletes a character from the line.
F1 or →	Copies one character from the preceding command line.
F2	Copies all characters from the preceding command line up to the next character you type.
F3	Copies all remaining characters from the preceding command line.
F4	Deletes all characters from the preceding command line up to, but not including, the next character typed (opposite of F2).
F5	Moves the current line into the buffer, but does not allow MS-DOS to execute the line.
F6	Produces an end-of-file marker when you copy from the console to a disk file.

Using DIR To View File Lists

The DIR command displays more than a list of file names. As your computing
expertise grows, you will find many uses for the information provided by the
full directory listing.

4

DOSSHELL is the
file name. The
file name is eight
characters long,
the limit for file-
name lengths.

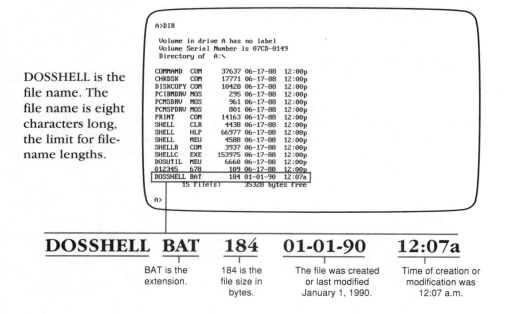

```
A>DIR

  Volume in drive A has no label
  Volume Serial Number is 07CD-0149
  Directory of  A:\

COMMAND  COM    37637 06-17-88  12:00p
CHKDSK   COM    17771 06-17-88  12:00p
DISKCOPY COM    10428 06-17-88  12:00p
PCIBMDRV MOS      295 06-17-88  12:00p
PCMSDRV  MOS      961 06-17-88  12:00p
PCMSPDRV MOS      801 06-17-88  12:00p
PRINT    COM    14163 06-17-88  12:00p
SHELL    CLR     4438 06-17-88  12:00p
SHELL    HLP    66977 06-17-88  12:00p
SHELL    MEU     4588 06-17-88  12:00p
SHELLB   COM     3937 06-17-88  12:00p
SHELLC   EXE   153975 06-17-88  12:00p
DOSUTIL  MEU     6660 06-17-88  12:00p
012345   678      109 06-17-88  12:00p
DOSSHELL BAT      184 01-01-90  12:07a
       15 File(s)      35328 bytes free

A>
```

DOSSHELL BAT	184	01-01-90	12:07a
BAT is the extension.	184 is the file size in bytes.	The file was created or last modified January 1, 1990.	Time of creation or modification was 12:07 a.m.

Defining the DIR Command

A directory is a list of files. With the DIR command, you get a volume label,
five columns of information about the files, and the amount of unused space
on the disk. Try the DIR command now. Type

DIR

and press Enter. You have just told DOS to list the files on the logged drive.
You can also type **DIR A:** to specify drive A or **DIR C:** to list the files on drive
C. The A and C are the drive parameters. If you don't specify a drive, DOS
uses the logged drive by default.

You can change the logged drive by typing a drive letter and a colon and pressing Enter. For example, by typing **A:** at the DOS prompt, you change the logged drive to drive A. A disk must be in a drive before DOS can make it the logged drive. You can log only to a real drive that your system contains. By changing the logged drive, you can switch between a hard disk and a floppy disk.

Controlling Scrolling

Scrolling describes how a screen fills with information. As the screen fills with information, the lines of the display scroll off the top of the screen. To stop a scrolling screen, you press the key combination Ctrl-S. Press any key to restart the scrolling. On enhanced keyboards, press the Pause key to stop the scrolling.

Examining the Directory Listing

The first line you see in the directory listing is the volume label. A volume label is an identification that you specify when you prepare the disk. The volume label is optional, but using one makes organizing your disks easier.

The next lines in the directory listing contain file information. Each line in the directory describes one file. You see the file name, extension, and size of file in bytes. You also see the date and time the file was created or last changed. Look at what this information means.

File Names and Extensions

The file name contains two parts: the name and the extension. A period delimits the file name and its extension. In the directory listing, however, spaces separate the file names and extensions.

In any single directory, each file must have a unique name. DOS treats the file name and the extension as two separate parts. The file names MYFILE.123 and MYFILE.ABC are unique because each file has a different extension. The file names MYFILE.123 and YOURFILE.123 are also unique. Many DOS commands make use of the two parts of the file name separately.

For this reason it is a good idea to give each file a file name and an extension.

File names should help you identify the contents of a file. DOS file names can contain only eight alphanumeric characters, plus a three-character extension. With this built-in limit, meeting the demand of uniqueness and meaningfulness needed for some file names can require ingenuity.

DOS is also specific about which characters you use in a file name or an extension. To be safe, use only letters of the alphabet and numbers, not spaces or a period. DOS truncates excess characters in a file name.

File Size and Date/Time Stamps

In the directory listing, the third column shows the size of the file in bytes. This measurement is an approximation of the size of your file. Your file can actually contain a somewhat fewer number of bytes than shown. Because computers reserve blocks of data storage for files, files with slightly different data amounts may have identical file-size listings. This disk-space allocation method also explains why your word processing memo with only five words can occupy 2K of file space.

The last two columns in the directory listing display a date and a time. These entries represent the time you created the file or, with an established file, the time you altered the file. Your computer's internal date and time are the basis for the date and time stamp in the directory. As you create more files, the date and time stamp become invaluable tools in determining the most recent version of a file.

The last line of the directory tells you the total number of files a disk contains and the amount of free space available. Free space is measured in bytes. Knowing the amount of free space is useful when you want to determine how many more files a disk can hold.

The Wild-Card Characters

Technically, the wild card is a character in a command that depicts one or more characters. In DOS, the question mark (?) character represents any single character. The * represents all characters in a file name. Although using commands seems complex, wild cards simplify many operations.

84

For example, although the command, COPY A:*.BAT C: /V, looks like hieroglyphics from an Egyptian tomb, all it says is this:

1. This is a copy function.
2. From the disk in drive A, copy everything (designated by the asterisk) that ends with the three-letter extension BAT.
3. Place a copy of these files in drive C.
4. And (represented by the /) verify that the copy is the same as the original.

Using Wild Cards in the DIR Command

You can use wild cards with the DIR command. The following text provides examples of the use of wild-card characters.

The long form of the DIR command looks like this:

DIR *d:filename.ext*

When you use DIR alone, DOS lists all files in the directory. When you use DIR with a file name and extension parameter, DOS lists files that match the parameter. Type the DIR command, for example, remembering to substitute an actual drive letter for the *d:*. In place of *filename.ext*, type **MYFILE.123**:

DIR MYFILE.123

The DIR command you just typed tells DOS to list a directory of all files matching MYFILE.123. The directory lists only one file, MYFILE.123.

If you want a listing of all files that have an extension of 123, type the following command:

DIR *.123

DOS lists any file in the logged directory that has a 123 extension. For example, the files MYFILE.123 and YOURFILE.123 would display.

If you issue the command

DIR MYFILE.*

you might get a listing of MYFILE.123 and MYFILE.XYZ.

You can give your letter files a LET extension and your memo files the extension MEM. This practice lets you use the DIR command with a wild card to get separate listings of the two types of files.

The ? wild card differs from the * wild card. Any character that is in the precise position as the ? is a match. If you issue the command DIR MYFILE?.123, files such as MYFILE1.123 and MYFILE2.123 appear, but MYFILE.123 doesn't. The same rules apply to other commands that allow wild cards.

4

Lessons Learned

- DOS requires accuracy in issuing commands, not because it is unfriendly, but because its syntax is limited. Don't be intimidated by the DOS command line.
- Although DOS has dozens of commands, you use fewer than 10 with any frequency.
- Fancy terms can have simple descriptions. For example, a *delimiter* is a character used as a separator.
- Wild cards are the shorthand of DOS commands. The asterisk (*) can stand for any number of characters, and the question mark (?) substitutes for one letter in a command.
- The DIR command lists files in a directory.
- A directory listing tells you the file name, size (in bytes), and time and date of last update.

Now, let's discuss the concept of DOS format.

The DOS Format

I remember my two favorite grade school days (neither involved report cards). One was the day just before summer recess. The other was day two of the new school year, when we bought loose-leaf binders, section sheets, tabs, and paper. There was something special about prying open those big chrome rings and arranging all the items necessary for organized note taking. The paper was lined and pristine, everything was sectioned off, and labels identifying subjects were written as neatly as small fingers allowed.

This little reminiscence suggests what Chapter 5 is about: preparing disks to hold and organize information. If nothing else, reading this chapter teaches you how to format any MS-DOS disk. The topics covered are formatting floppy disks, assigning volume labels, transferring system files, and understanding FORMAT error messages.

Learning how to format disks is easy if you accept the role of the patient student. The agreeable part of formatting disks is that DOS does it all. You don't even have to worry about poor penmanship.

> **Key Terms Used in This Chapter**
>
> | | |
> |---|---|
> | *Format* | Initial preparation of a disk for data storage. |
> | *Volume* | A disk-level name that identifies a particular disk. |
> | *Track* | A circular section of a disk's surface that holds data. |
> | *Sector* | A section of a track that acts as the disk's smallest storage unit. |
> | *Internal command* | A DOS command built into COMMAND.COM. |
> | *External command* | A DOS command located in a separate DOS file and loaded by COMMAND.COM before being executed. |

Understanding the FORMAT Command

A floppy disk is a Mylar pancake in a plastic dust cover. The Mylar disk is covered with magnetic material similar to the metallic coating on recording tape. Out of the box, disks aren't ready for you to use. You must *format* them first.

DOS's FORMAT command performs the preparation process for disks. You simply enter the command, and FORMAT analyzes for disk defects, generates a root directory, sets up a storage table, and alters other parts of the disk.

The magnetic disk is like unlined paper—hardly a good medium for proper magnetic penmanship. Although blank pages are fine for writing casual notes, you could wind up with wandering, uneven script. Lines on the paper serve as guides to help keep you on track.

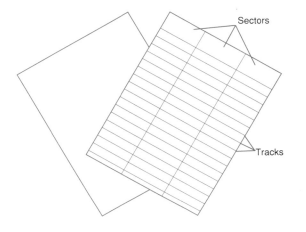

Formatted disks can be compared to lined paper, with horizontal lines subdivided by vertical lines.

5

As lines on paper are guides for the writer, tracks and sectors on a disk are guides for the computer. Because the storage medium of a spinning disk is circular, the "premarked lines," or magnetic divisions called *tracks*, are placed in concentric circles. These tracks are further subdivided into areas called *sectors*.

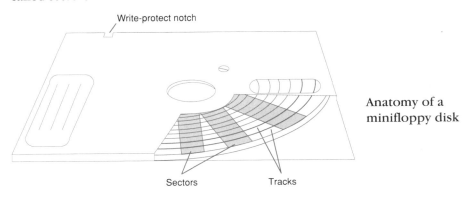

Anatomy of a minifloppy disk

When you format a blank disk, DOS *encodes*—or programs—tracks and sectors onto the disk surface. DOS decides what type of drive you have and then positions the tracks and sectors accordingly. DOS stores data in these sectors and uses both the track and sector number to find and retrieve information.

A standard floppy disk (one that holds 360K of data) has 40 tracks per side. A standard microfloppy disk (720K) has 80 tracks per side. Higher-capacity disks have more tracks and more sectors.

As formatting your disks becomes a routine task, remember to use care. Formatting erases *all* information that a disk contains. If you format a disk you have used earlier, everything stored on that disk disappears. Be careful not to format disks holding files you want to keep. Labeling your disks helps you avoid such a mishap. Another precaution is to write-protect disks that hold important information—by adding tape tabs on 5 1/4-inch disks or setting the write-protect switch on 3 1/2-inch disks.

In any case, you should use the DIR command to inspect the files that disk holds before you try to format a used floppy. Using DIR is like reviewing what you've written on a blackboard before erasing it.

5

Formatting Floppy Disks

The process of formatting floppy disks varies, depending on the number of drives in your system. Because FORMAT is an external command, COMMAND.COM must load it from a working DOS disk (or from the hard disk). The DOS V4.0 installation process creates a working DOS disk. If you have an earlier DOS version, use a working copy of the System disk wherever you are asked to insert the working DOS disk.

Before you begin, you should have a floppy disk ready to format. To avoid mistaking formatted disks for unformatted disks, place an indicator on the label of each disk you format. The indicator may be as simple as a dot, a check mark, or the letter F for *formatted*. Throughout the steps in this section, you are asked to use a more literal identifier: the word *formatted*.

To prepare a floppy disk for formatting:

1. Write *formatted* on the label of the disk.
2. Insert the working DOS disk into the proper drive. (If DOS is installed on the hard disk in your computer, skip this step.)
3. Boot your computer, following the instructions for your system.
4. Use one of the following FORMAT directions that conforms to your hardware's setup of disk drives.

Formatting on a Single Floppy Disk Drive System

Using the FORMAT command is straightforward on computers that have only one floppy disk drive. To format a disk, follow these steps:

1. Close the drive door if necessary.
2. Type **FORMAT B:** **/V** and press ⏎Enter)

A single floppy disk drive serves as both drive A and drive B.

After you type the command to format the disk, a message appears, similar to the one shown here.

3. Replace the working DOS disk in drive A with the disk you labeled *formatted*.
4. Press ⏎Enter)

91

When you press Enter, the indicator light on the drive glows as the formatting process begins.

Warning: Versions of DOS before V3.0 do not require that you specify the drive that holds the disk you want to format. If you simply issue the FORMAT command with no drive parameter, and the logged disk holds the DOS working copy, DOS attempts to format the working copy. If you write-protect your DOS working copy, however, FORMAT cannot harm it.

Formatting on a Two Floppy Disk Drive System

Formatting disks on two floppy disk drive systems is nearly as simple as formatting disks on single floppy drive systems. As presented in the preceding section, follow these steps to format a disk:

1. Close the drive door if necessary.
2. Type **FORMAT B:** and press ⏎Enter). If your DOS version is earlier than 4.XX, type **FORMAT B:** /V and press ⏎Enter)
3. Insert the disk labeled *formatted* into drive B.
4. Press ⏎Enter)

Formatting on a Hard Disk Drive System

Hard disks are a wonder! Besides being capable of holding and accessing large quantities of data at high speed, hard disks end playing musical chairs with your DOS disk or disks. Because COMMAND.COM and all of the DOS utility files are immediately accessible, you need only to decide which drive you want to use to format a floppy disk.

If you have only one floppy disk drive (and no hard drive), you really have no decision to make. The default designation is always drive A. If you have two floppy drives, you can use either drive A or B.

To format a floppy disk on a hard disk drive system, follow these steps:

1. Check to see that drive C is your logged disk drive and that the C> prompt is displayed.
2. For DOS V4.0 or later, type **FORMAT A:** and press ⏎Enter). For DOS versions earlier than 4.XX, type **FORMAT A:** /V and press ⏎Enter)

This command allows you to format a floppy disk in drive A.

5

3. Insert the disk labeled *formatted* in drive A.
4. Press ⏎Enter

Looking at the FORMAT Command's Output

Versions of DOS earlier than V4.0 show the track and sector numbers as formatting proceeds. With DOS V4.0, the FORMAT command gives you the percentage of the disk that has been formatted. When the formatting process is complete, you see the following message:

```
Format complete
Volume label (11 characters, ENTER for none)?
```

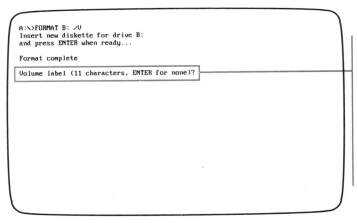

You are then prompted to enter a volume label if you have issued FORMAT with the /V switch. V4.0 users see this report automatically.

You can give the disk a volume name of up to 11 characters, or you can press Enter to omit the volume name. Remember that, with DOS V4.0, the volume label switch is automatic.

Next, a report is displayed about the capacity of your diskette. The report shows the total disk space and total bytes available on the disk. If FORMAT detects *bad sectors*—that is, bad spots—on the disk, it marks them as unusable. FORMAT also reports how many bytes are unavailable because of bad sectors. DOS V4.0 displays how many bytes each *allocation unit* (sector) contains, and how many allocation units are available for storage on the disk.

The DOS V4.0 report for a 1.44M formatted disk.

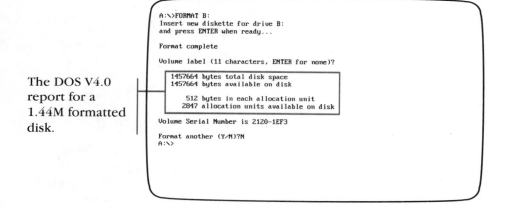

```
A:\>FORMAT B:
Insert new diskette for drive B:
and press ENTER when ready...

Format complete

Volume label (11 characters, ENTER for none)?

  1457664 bytes total disk space
  1457664 bytes available on disk

      512 bytes in each allocation unit
     2847 allocation units available on disk

Volume Serial Number is 2120-1EF3

Format another (Y/N)?N
A:\>
```

The numbers for various sizes of disks vary, as shown in the following figures.

A report for a for-matted 360K floppy disk.

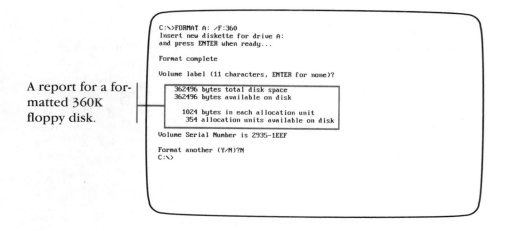

```
C:\>FORMAT A: /F:360
Insert new diskette for drive A:
and press ENTER when ready...

Format complete

Volume label (11 characters, ENTER for none)?

  362496 bytes total disk space
  362496 bytes available on disk

    1024 bytes in each allocation unit
     354 allocation units available on disk

Volume Serial Number is 2935-1EEF

Format another (Y/N)?N
C:\>
```

94

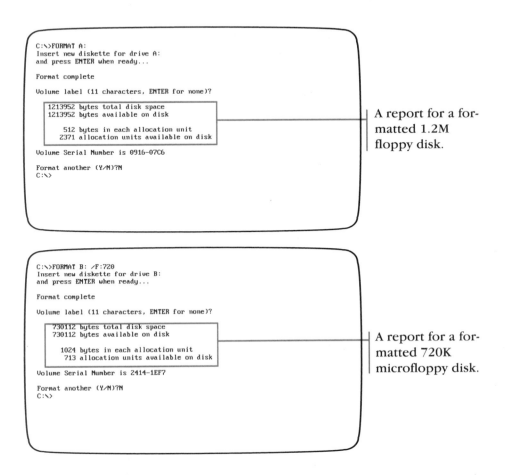

```
C:\>FORMAT A:
Insert new diskette for drive A:
and press ENTER when ready...

Format complete

Volume label (11 characters, ENTER for none)?
    1213952 bytes total disk space
    1213952 bytes available on disk

        512 bytes in each allocation unit
       2371 allocation units available on disk

Volume Serial Number is 0916-07C6

Format another (Y/N)?N
C:\>
```

A report for a formatted 1.2M floppy disk.

```
C:\>FORMAT B: /F:720
Insert new diskette for drive B:
and press ENTER when ready...

Format complete

Volume label (11 characters, ENTER for none)?
    730112 bytes total disk space
    730112 bytes available on disk

      1024 bytes in each allocation unit
       713 allocation units available on disk

Volume Serial Number is 2414-1EF7

Format another (Y/N)?N
C:\>
```

A report for a formatted 720K microfloppy disk.

The last part of the report prompts for additional formatting activity:

    FORMAT another? (Y/N)?

By answering Yes to the prompt and pressing Enter, you can format another disk while the FORMAT program is loaded in system RAM. Answering No returns you to the DOS command prompt.

Learning FORMAT's Switch Options

As with many DOS commands, you can add switches to modify the FORMAT command. If you separate the switch from the command with the slash (/)

95

character, you can add more than one switch to some commands. For example, **FORMAT B:** /V/S is a valid command.

The /V (Volume Label) Switch

DOS reserves a few bytes of data space on disks so that you can place an electronic identification, called a *volume label*, on each disk. Think of a volume label for a disk in the same context as the volume number of a book. You must use the /V switch to assign a volume label if you use a version of DOS earlier than 4.0. Version 4.0 automatically includes the /V switch as part of the FORMAT command.

When you assign a volume label, you can use the following characters, in any order:

- Letters A to Z and a to z
- Numerals 0 to 9
- Special characters and punctuation symbols:

    ~ ! @ # $ ^ & ( ) – _ { } '
- A space character (V3.3 and later)

When you enter too many characters, or an illegal character, in the volume name, DOS V3.3 (and later versions) uses only the characters you typed, up to the mistake. Earlier DOS versions ask you for the volume label again. If you do not want to name the disk, just press Enter.

The /S (Transfer System Files) Switch

The /S switch places the DOS system files on the formatted disk. Use this switch if you want to be able to boot your PC with the disk you are formatting. You cannot see these hidden files in the directory of the disk, but the files are there, along with COMMAND.COM.

Placing the operating system on a disk has both advantages and drawbacks. On the positive side, you can always boot your system from any disk containing the operating system. On the negative side, the /S switch reduces the available storage capacity of the disk by about 80K.

Use the following syntax for this command:

   FORMAT *d:* /S

96

Remember to replace *d:* with the appropriate drive letter. You will almost always use A or B to format a floppy disk.

If you have one floppy disk drive, your computer acts as though drive A is both drive A and drive B. The FORMAT command also treats your single floppy drive as both drive A and B.

If you have two floppy disk drives, DOS formats the disk in drive B with system files. If you are using a hard disk, DOS formats the floppy disk in drive A.

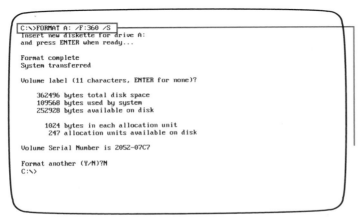

```
C:\>FORMAT A: /F:360 /S
Insert new diskette for drive A:
and press ENTER when ready...

Format complete
System transferred

Volume label (11 characters, ENTER for none)?

    362496 bytes total disk space
    109568 bytes used by system
    252928 bytes available on disk

      1024 bytes in each allocation unit
       247 allocation units available on disk

Volume Serial Number is 2052-07C7

Format another (Y/N)?N
C:\>
```

The report for a 360K disk formatted with system files.

Many newcomers to the PC copy the operating system to every disk they format. As you gain experience, and if your system has a hard disk drive, you will rarely use the /S switch.

The /4 (Reduce Capacity) Switch

The /4 switch allows you to format a disk in a high-capacity disk drive for double-sided disk drive use. Use this switch to prepare a disk in a 1.2M drive for use in a 360K drive. Note: Despite the provision for downward compatibility, disks prepared this way are often not readable on the 360K drive.

The Other Switches

Primarily, the /1, /8, /B, /N, and /T FORMAT switches allow current versions of DOS to format disks for early computers or for computers that use the first versions of DOS. Although you may never need to use these switches, a brief description of each will help you better understand their functions.

/1 tells DOS to prepare a single-sided disk for use in a single-sided disk drive. /8 prepares a disk with 8 sectors per track. /B allows room for the system files on an 8-sectors-per-track disk. /N and /T allow you to vary the number of tracks and sectors on high-capacity disks.

5 Understanding FORMAT and the Logged Drive

Earlier in the book, you learned how a single alphabetical letter followed by a colon designates a disk drive. When this combination is used in a command, DOS interprets the letter and the colon as the disk specifier. You also learned how to use the DIR command, without the drive specifier, on the command line. In this case, DOS assumes that you want a directory for the previously logged drive.

As with DIR, you can use FORMAT even if it is not on the logged drive, but because FORMAT is an external command, you must take an extra step. For example, if FORMAT is on drive C, the logged drive is A, and you want to format a disk in drive B, type the following after the A> prompt:

   C:FORMAT B:

where **C:** is the added step that tells DOS where the external command is located, and **B** is the disk you want formatted.

Understanding Default Values

DOS uses certain prepackaged, or default, values to carry out its services. You can override many of these values through commands or switches. Some values, such as the /S switch for FORMAT, remain in effect for only one instance. Changing other defaults, such as the logged drive, causes the default to change to the new value.

DOS normally displays the default drive name at the DOS prompt and uses this drive to execute commands. If the drive specifier is the same as the default drive, you do not have to enter the drive letter. If you want to issue a command to another disk drive, you must enter the drive specifier for that disk in the command line. The command is shorter and cleaner if you exclude the defaults. Many command examples you use in this book assume some default values. The logged drive is a frequently used default.

When you boot your computer, DOS displays the name of the drive that holds the DOS disk from which you booted, such as

```
C>
```

This drive is the default (or current, or logged) drive.

Using FORMAT on Another Drive

You remember that COMMAND.COM contains built-in DOS commands, called internal commands. External DOS commands reside on disk. COMMAND.COM must find and load external commands before executing them. If the external commands are not on the disk in the logged drive, you must enter a drive specifier *before* the command name. The drive specifier is the name of the drive that contains the command's program file. Chapter 6 explains how to give DOS the correct path to the external commands.

Suppose, for example, that you are formatting a disk in drive B. With DOS loaded in drive A and a blank disk in drive B, type **A:**. Press Enter to make the drive holding the DOS working disk your default drive. Then type **FORMAT B:** to format the blank disk in drive B.

If you change to drive B and enter the FORMAT B: command, you see an error message. Because drive B is not the default drive, DOS can't find FORMAT.COM.

One solution to this dilemma is to issue the command **A:FORMAT B:**. DOS finds the FORMAT command on the DOS disk in drive A as specified in the command. The formatting is done on the blank disk in drive B, as specified in the command.

The FORMAT command in DOS versions V3.0 and later requires that you specify the drive for the disk to be formatted, even if the drive is the default.

5

99

Prior DOS versions don't require you to name the drive in the command. Be careful not to format the wrong disk by default!

To issue an external command to be executed from another disk drive, enter the drive letter for that disk drive before you type the command name.

In this example, the FORMAT program is on the disk in drive A, and the disk to be formatted is in drive B. The logged drive is C.

```
C:\>A:FORMAT B:
```

Working with Internal and External Commands

You can subdivide DOS commands into two groups: *internal* and *external* commands, as shown in tables 5.1 and 5.2.

Table 5.1
Internal DOS Commands

BREAK	DEL	RMDIR
CHCP	DIR	SET
CHDIR	ERASE	TIME
CLS	MKDIR	TYPE
COPY	PATH	VER
CTTY	PROMPT	VERIFY
DATE	RENAME	VOL

100

Table 5.2
Common External DOS Commands

APPEND	DOSSHELL	SORT
ASSIGN	FIND	SYS
BACKUP	FORMAT	TREE
CHDSK	PRINT	XCOPY
DISKCOMP	MORE	
DISKCOPY	RESTORE	

Don't be disturbed by the number of external commands because few of them are used with any frequency. Also, don't try memorizing them. Reference manuals are designed to free you from getting swamped by information you rarely use. External commands contained in different versions of DOS vary.

With external commands, such as FORMAT, DOS prompts you to place the proper disk into the drive before it carries out the command. If you have a floppy disk system, you can remove the DOS working copy that contains FORMAT, insert the disk you want to format, and press any key.

Understanding FORMAT's Error Messages

The most common DOS error messages are rarely catastrophes. They are little more than statements suggesting that you did something wrong. Take them seriously because they do show that, for a particular reason, your commands won't be carried out. On the other hand, some error messages indicate a serious problem. Chapter 12 explains the most important error messages.

With floppy disks, errors that occur during formatting activity are usually not serious. For example, if you insert a blank disk into the drive where DOS expects to find the FORMAT command *before* you issue the FORMAT command, DOS displays an error message.

This message may indicate an incorrectly formatted disk, a disk that is incompatible with the drive, or a damaged disk.

Format the disk again, making sure that the disk is formatted for your system. If the disk is damaged, replace it.

Some disks do not format properly the first time. If, after the second format attempt, the general failure message is still present, you may want to use a different disk.

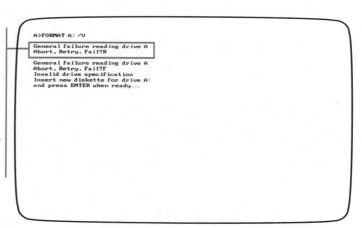

When DOS cannot find the internal file tables on the blank disk when it tries to load FORMAT, it assumes that the disk, the drive, or the drive electronics failed.

The solution is to place the DOS disk in the drive and answer the prompt **R** to retry. If the retry fails, substitute another disk.

102

When you insert and remove disks during formatting sessions, you can give DOS the "go ahead" too soon when you are prompted to Press any key when ready. When you make this error, DOS displays the message:

```
Not Ready Error Reading in Drive A
Abort, Retry, Fail?
```

If the preceding error occurs during the FORMAT process, DOS displays an error message.

To try again, remove the disk and reinsert it, close the drive door if necessary, and issue the FORMAT command again. Abort the operation by typing **A**. To recover, make sure that the disk is properly inserted in the drive, close the drive door. Enter **R** at the prompt.

5

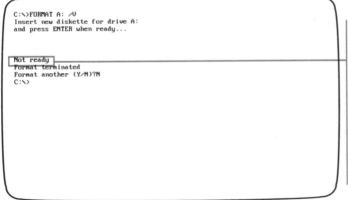

```
C:\>FORMAT A: /U
Insert new diskette for drive A:
and press ENTER when ready...


Not ready
Format terminated
Format another (Y/N)?N
C:\>
```

DOS couldn't read from the disk drive. The drive door may be open (not un-common when you swap disks in and out of floppy drives), or the disk may not be inserted.

Another kind of error involves a write-protection problem.

103

```
C:\>FORMAT A: /V
Insert new diskette for drive A:
and press ENTER when ready...

Write protect error
Format terminated
Format another (Y/N)?N
C:\>
```

This error occurred when DOS tried to format a write-protected disk. Write protection saved the disk from accidental erasure.

5

To format a write-protected disk (if you really want to), simply remove the write-protection from the disk and attempt a second format.

The first three error conditions arise during formatting, and the fourth is a common user error, but these conditions can happen when you use other DOS commands. These errors are not FORMAT errors. Because FORMAT is an external command and FORMAT acts primarily on blank disks, these errors are likely to occur.

If the FORMAT command detects unusable areas on the disk, you will see a line describing the problem in the report. For example, the line might state `430,000 bytes in bad sectors`.

```
C:\>FORMAT A: /V
Insert new diskette for drive A:
and press ENTER when ready...

Format complete

Volume label (11 characters, ENTER for none)?
     1213952 bytes total disk space
      430080 bytes in bad sectors
      783872 bytes available on disk

         512 bytes in each allocation unit
        1531 allocation units available on disk

Volume Serial Number is 3F6B-07D9

Format another (Y/N)?N
C:\>
```

Bad sectors can sometimes cause trouble when DOS tries to read a disk.

104

Although not a true error message, a bad-sectors report points out a possible problem with the disk.

The bytes in bad sectors message means that MS-DOS found bad sectors on the disk. These sectors cannot be used to hold information. The total amount of free space on the disk is reduced by the number of bytes in the bad sectors.

Try reformatting the disk. If it still has bad sectors, you can have your dealer replace the disk, or you can use the disk as is. Before you do either, though, try formatting the disk again.

The worst disk-error message is

    Invalid media or track 0 bad – disk unusable

5

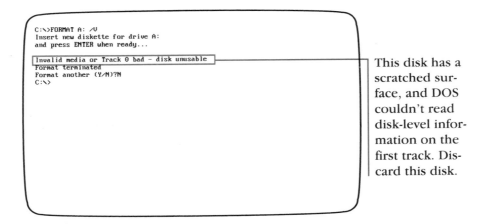

```
C:\>FORMAT A: /V
Insert new diskette for drive A:
and press ENTER when ready...

Invalid media or Track 0 bad – disk unusable
Format terminated
Format another (Y/N)?N
C:\>
```

This disk has a scratched surface, and DOS couldn't read disk-level information on the first track. Discard this disk.

This message may mean that the areas on the disk that hold key DOS system data are bad. If you get the disk unusable error message on a new disk, take it back to your dealer. If the disk is old, throw it away. Disks are inexpensive and, in this case, should be discarded. Trying to use a bad disk is being penny-wise and pound-foolish.

An Invalid media message also stems from using a disk whose capacity is wrong for your computer system. The methods used to prepare disk surfaces when formatting the various capacity drives differ. Using a higher capacity disk than necessary, for example, can cause disk errors.

Some systems are set up with a RAM disk. A RAM disk is a portion of system memory that software treats collectively as a disk drive. RAM disks are also called *virtual disks* or *memory disks*. You cannot format a RAM disk.

Cautions about Formatting a Hard Disk

Many computer dealers install the operating system on a computer's hard disk before you receive it. If your dealer has installed an applications program, such as a word processor, *do not format the hard disk. If you reformat your hard disk, all programs and data will be erased*.

Hard disks are a desirable part of a computer system because of their speed and storage capacity. And, just like floppy disks, they must be formatted before you use them. Unless you are familiar with the procedure, however, **DO NOT ATTEMPT TO FORMAT YOUR HARD DISK!**

Should you ever attempt to reformat your hard disk, first perform a complete back-up. Make sure that you are familiar with the RESTORE command (see Chapter 8). You also should have a bootable floppy disk ready that contains a copy of RESTORE. The *MS-DOS User's Guide,* Special Edition, devotes several pages to preparing and formatting a hard disk. If you must format your hard disk, consult that book or your computer's manual.

Remember that FORMAT erases all data that a disk contains. Always check the directory of the disk you want to format. It may hold data you need. Make a mental note to check the command line thoroughly when you use the FORMAT command. For example, if you are accustomed to typing **C:** as a drive specifier, habit might lead you into a disastrous FORMAT mistake.

Using a software program designed to improve your hard disk's performance is a better and safer alternative than formatting. Disk Optimizer is one such program, but other good programs exist. Ask your computer hardware or software dealer which program is the best one for your system.

Lessons Learned

- Unformatted floppy disks can be compared to sheets of unlined paper.
- Formatting a disk is analogous to lining off your notepad before writing.
- You have the ability to label your work.
- When formatting, two disk drives are more convenient than one.
- Internal commands are built into COMMAND.COM, whereas external commands are separate programs that instruct COMMAND.COM.
- Don't try to memorize every DOS command. Most of them are rarely, if ever, used.
- Error messages can be helpful. Most of them do not indicate impending catastrophe.
- Hard disks demand special treatment and care when the FORMAT command is used.

Now, let's look at DOS's roots and directory tree.

5

107

5

Discovering DOS's Roots

Have you ever noticed how some people never get lost, and others spend half their lives stopping at gas stations to ask for directions? Some people have the enviable talent of finding their way around, almost as though the genes of a bloodhound were hiding somewhere in the obscurity of their ancestry.

Most of us lack the built-in compass, sharp vision, or sensitive sense of smell of those lucky few. You've long known that maps make trips more pleasurable. True, it is annoying to refold a map at rest areas, but it's better than pulling into service stations when you don't need fuel. Nobody likes being in a strange land, at the mercy of a stranger's instructions.

Before the oil crisis of the 1970s, you could stop at any service station and pick up a free map. In fact, one oil company even provided travel routes. All you did was write to a special address, tell the oil company where you planned to go, and within a few weeks a map arrived showing both the quickest and the most scenic routes. DOS's directory structure provides something resembling that kind of personal touch.

Key Terms Used in this Chapter

Hierarchical directory	An organizational structure used by DOS to segregate files into levels of subdirectories.
Tree structure	A term applied to hierarchical directories to describe the concept in which directories "belong" to higher directories, and "own" lower directories. Viewed graphically, the ownership relationships resemble an inverted tree.
Directory	An area of the DOS file system holding information about files and directories. The root directory is the highest directory of the tree structure of DOS. All DOS disks have a root directory, automatically created by DOS (versions 2.0 and later).
Subdirectory	A directory created within another directory, and subordinate to that directory. Also called, simply, a directory.
Directory specifier	A DOS command parameter, telling DOS where to find a file or where to carry out a command.
Path name	Another name for the directory specifier. The path name gives DOS the directions it needs to trace the directory tree to the directory containing desired commands or files.
Backslash (\)	The character DOS expects to see in a command to separate directory names. Used alone as a parameter, the backslash signifies the root directory.
PATH command	The command that instructs DOS to search through a specified set of directories for files having COM, EXE, and BAT extensions. DOS searches the path if the selected command, executable, or batch file can't be found in the current directory.

6

The DOS Directory Concept

Despite what you hear, DOS doesn't strand you on the road without a map. Understandably, people beginning to use a PC don't know the "proper address" to write to for the scenic or direct routes. This chapter is designed to be your map to DOS.

In Chapter 4, you used the DIR command to list the contents of a disk directory. A directory is more than a file list displayed on a screen. It is also part of an internal software listing that DOS stores in a magnetic index on the disk. A poorly structured disk directory turns any hard drive into a bewildering tangle of misplaced files.

This chapter explains DOS's hierarchical, directory structure. Here, you discover how to use DOS to group and organize files and how to use the PATH command to move easily around your hard disk. You will also learn how DOS commands help you logically organize your disk directory.

6

Navigating a Hard Disk's Directories

DOS uses directories to organize files on a disk. A directory listing contains file information—the name, size, and creation or revision date for each file. Computer operators use the directory of a disk to find specific files. DOS also uses some or all of this directory information to service requests for data stored in the files on disks.

All MS-DOS-based disks have at least one directory. One directory is usually adequate for a floppy disk. Because floppy disks have relatively limited capacities, the number of files that fit on a floppy is limited. Hard disks, on the other hand, have very large storage capacities. A fixed disk can contain hundreds or even thousands of files. Without some form of organization, you will waste time sifting and sorting through your disk's directories to find a specific file.

Although floppy disks can use DOS's multiple directory structure, this feature is more important for extending order to the storage capacity of hard disks. With a bit of foresight, you can store your files in fewer, more logically grouped directories so you (and DOS) can more easily locate your files.

Versions of MS-DOS starting with V2.0 incorporate the *hierarchical directory system*. This means that one directory leads to another, which can lead to another, and so on. This multilevel file structure lets you create a filing system for your files. Hierarchical directories are like the library's system of storing books and breaking them out by ever-narrower subject categories.

Computer people use the term *tree structure* to describe the organization of files into hierarchical levels of directories. Try picturing the tree structure as an inverted tree. You can visualize the file system with the first-level directory as the root or trunk of the tree. The trunk branches into major limbs to the next level of directories under the root. These directories branch into other directories. Directories have files, like leaves, attached to them. The terms *directory* and *subdirectory* are interchangeable.

6

DOS's directory structure, viewed as a tree-structure hierarchy. The root directory is the topmost directory.

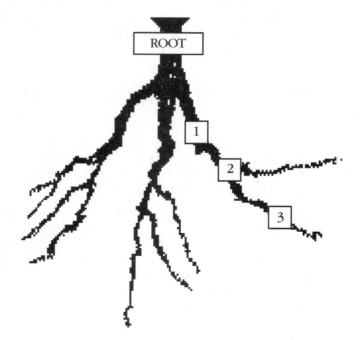

112

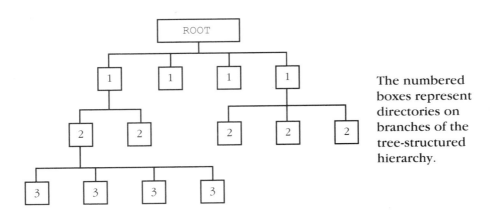

The numbered boxes represent directories on branches of the tree-structured hierarchy.

The tree-structure analogy loses some of its neatness when it is expanded to cover the capabilities of the hierarchical directory structure. This is because any directory, except the root, can have as many subdirectories as space on the disk allows. Depending on the disk drive, the root directory can handle a preset number of subdirectories. 360K minifloppies hold 112 entries and 1.2M minifloppies handle 224 entries in the root directory. 720K and 1.4M microfloppies can hold, respectively, 112 and 224 entries. Hard disks have a typical root directory capacity of 512 entries.

When you format a disk, DOS creates a main directory for that disk. This directory is called the *root* directory. The root directory is the default directory until you change to another directory. DOS designates the root directory with the backslash (\) character. You cannot delete the root directory.

A subdirectory is any directory excluding the root directory. A subdirectory can contain data files as well as other, lower subdirectories. Subdirectory names must conform to the naming rules for DOS files, but subdirectory names normally do not have extensions. It is a good idea to name subdirectories for the type of files they contain. In this way, you can remember what type of files each subdirectory contains.

6

The terms directory and subdirectory are frequently used interchangeably. A subdirectory of the root can have its own subdirectories. By naming the branches, you can describe where you are working in the tree structure. You simply start at the root and name each branch that leads to your current branch.

Disk directories are also frequently called "parent" and "child" directories. You can compare this structure to that of a diversified corporation with numerous subsidiaries. Each "child" of the parent can have "children" of its own. In the directory hierarchy, each directory's "parent" is the directory just above it.

6

A corporate com-
mand structure
is similar to the
disk directory
concept.

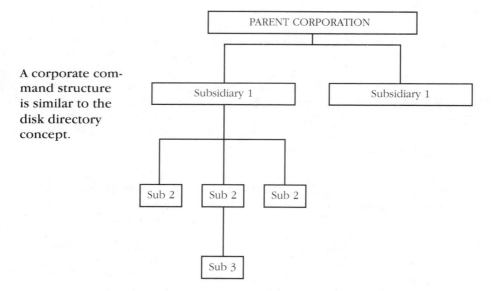

Directories do not share information about their contents with other directories. In a way, each subdirectory acts as a disk within a bigger disk. This idea of privacy extends to the DOS commands that you issue. The directory structure allows DOS commands to act on the contents of the current directory and leave other directories undisturbed.

When you issue a command that specifies a file, but not a directory, DOS looks for that file in the default, or current, directory. You can access any point in the tree structure and remain at your current directory.

When you think about it, the tree analogy isn't easy to envision. The inverted tree concept is as awkward as picturing the Empire State Building torn from its base and turned upside down. You can think of the building's foundation as the root directory, and the exposed plumbing as subdirectories, but the image is still awkward.

Then again, there is an organic logic to the tree analogy. Any squirrel will tell you that you can't reach the farthermost branch of a limb without starting from the limb nearest the base. From there, the limb branches off to several others. They, in turn, branch off still further. The important thing to note is that no more than one limb can be used to reach any of the limb's potentially numerous branches.

Consider a directory path as a series of stopping points on the way to a destination.

Paths in the Tree Structure

Before DOS can locate a file in the tree structure, it must know where to find the file. The *directory specifier* simply tells DOS in which directory a certain file resides. DOS must know the drive you want to use, the directory name, and the name of the file. In the command line, you type the disk drive, the directory name, and finally, the file name. DOS uses this information to find and act on the file.

Path Names

You can compare DOS to a corporate empire that has an extremely strict order of command. All communications must "go through channels." If, for example, a subsidiary at level 3 wants to communicate with the parent corporation, the message must go through both subsidiary 2 and 1. In DOS, this routing is called a *path*.

6

115

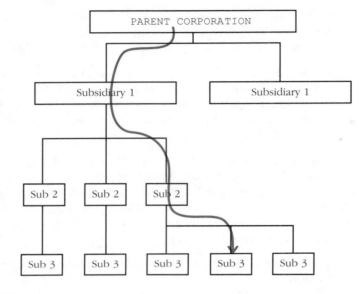

The parent cor-
poration is
analgous to the
root directory
and the subsid-
iaries are analo-
gous to
subdirectories.

6

A *path name* is a chain of directory names that tells DOS how to find the file
you want. To create a path name chain, you type the drive name, a subdirectory name (or sequence of subdirectory names), and the file name.
Make sure that you separate subdirectory names from each other with a
backslash (\) character. Using symbolic notation, the path name looks like
this:

   d:\directory\directory. . .\filename.ext

In this notation, *d:* is the drive letter. If you omit the drive specifier, DOS
uses the logged drive as the default drive. The *directory\directory. . .* names
the directories you want to search. The ellipsis (. . .) simply means that you
can add other directories to the specifier list. If you omit the directory
specifier from the path name, DOS assumes that you want to use the current
directory.

filename.ext is the name of the file. Notice that you use a \ to separate
directory names and the file name. The path name fully describes to DOS
where to direct its search for the file.

Use the following simple directory setup to understand directory paths in
DOS. Each subdirectory in this sample is a subdirectory of the root directory.

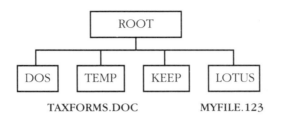

The subdirectory called LOTUS has a data file, MYFILE.123. Another subdirectory, TEMP, has a file called TAXFORMS.DOC.

MYFILE.123 is a data file in the LOTUS subdirectory. The complete path name for this file is the chain of directories that tells DOS how to find MYFILE.123. In this case, the chain consists of just two directories: the root (\) and LOTUS. The path name is

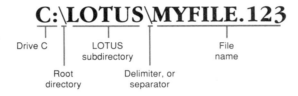

The path name for the TAXFORMS.DOC file is

Where the Search Starts

When you type a path name, DOS searches in the first specified directory. Then, it passes through the other specified directory branches to the file. The root directory has no name and is represented by the backslash (\). All directories grow from the root directory. If you want the search path to start at the root directory, begin the directory specification with a \. DOS begins its search for the file in the root and follows the subdirectory chain you include in the command.

6

Suppose that you want to see the directory listing for a budget file created by your Lotus 1-2-3 program. You might type a DIR command to give DOS a path similar to the following:

    DIR C:\LOTUS\DATA\BUDGET.WKS

DOS searches on drive C, beginning with the root directory, proceeds to the LOTUS subdirectory, and then arrives at the DATA subdirectory. If you omit the \ root name designator, DOS searches for files in your current directory.

The search starts in your current directory, not the root directory. DOS uses the path to your current directory as its default. If the current directory doesn't lead to the subdirectory that contains the file, you will receive a `file not found` error message. However, if the current directory contains the subdirectory, you do not have to type all the directory names in the path. In the preceding example, the current directory is C:\LOTUS. You can see the listing for the budget file with the following command:

    DIR DATA\BUDGET.WKS

Exploring Sample Subdirectories

Although you may not know what kind of directory organization you need, now is a good time to give some thought to establishing your directory tree. If your computer is part of a network, check with the network administrator before you make any changes.

The Root Directory

DOS creates the root directory for you, but you control which files to include in the root. The root is the top directory in the inverted tree. As a general rule, you should avoid cluttering the root directory with files.

The following diagram and the File System screen in the DOS V4.0 Shell illustrate the structure of a simple directory system. The structure consists of four directories, each a subdirectory of the root directory.

6

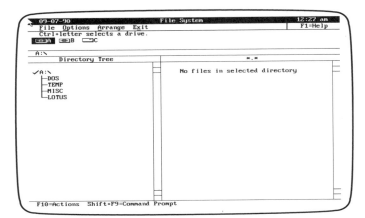

A variety of arrangements for the directory structure is possible.

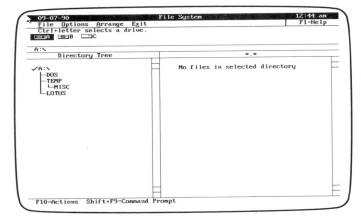

Many users find that two levels of subdirectories are sufficient.

Because the root is the default directory for DOS when you boot your system, COMMAND.COM. should be included in the root directory. DOS expects to find COMMAND.COM in the current directory when you boot. If DOS cannot load COMMAND.COM, DOS cannot communicate with you. DOS only manages to warn you that it cannot find the command interpreter.

In addition to COMMAND.COM, the root directory probably contains AUTOEXEC.BAT and CONFIG.SYS files. You will learn about these files in Chapter 10.

119

The AUTOEXEC.BAT file usually contains the PATH command that sets the search paths automatically. The root directory also contains the primary subdirectories for your computer. If your disk has no subdirectories, you add the first one to the root directory.

The \DOS Directory

You should create a \DOS directory and include it in your PATH command. All the utility files from your original DOS disks should be copied into this directory. You then have all your DOS functions grouped into one directory.

The \TEMP Directory

Many users find that they need a directory to store temporary files. You might find a directory named \TEMP useful. You can copy files to \TEMP as a temporary storage place until you copy the files to a more appropriate directory. A \TEMP directory is also useful for making copies of floppies in a single floppy, low-memory system.

You can copy files from the source disk to the \TEMP directory and then copy them back to the destination disk. If you have a single floppy drive, this copy method keeps you from swapping disks in and out of the single floppy drive.

Do not use the \TEMP directory as a permanent home for a file, however. You should be able to use a wild card to erase the directory periodically. This keeps the \TEMP directory empty for later use.

The \MISC or \KEEP Directory

You may have files in different directories that are no longer active, but feel you may still need them. Inactive files in a directory tend to increase clutter and make sorting through the directory confusing. With a \MISC or a \KEEP directory, you have an easily remembered home for those inactive files. Of course, you should delete only those files that are obviously of no more use to you.

Applications Software Directories

Many applications packages create directories when you install them on your hard disk. But if no directory is created by a program, it's a good idea to create one with a name that suggests the software name. For example, you might name your spreadsheet directory LOTUS. You can then copy the 1-2-3 package's files to the directory.

Commands To Manage Hard Disk Drive Maps

The examples presented so far in this chapter provide information on the structure of hierarchical directories. The following commands relate to your directory system's maintenance and use. These DOS directory commands consist of command names and parameters. With directory commands, you can customize your file system and navigate through it.

6

The MKDIR Command

To add a directory to your disk, use the MKDIR command. This command name has two names: MKDIR and MD. The command names are interchangeable. MKDIR means MaKe DIRectory. MD is an abbreviated name for the make directory command. Decide on a name for your proposed new directory. Use the MKDIR command at the DOS prompt in the form:

MKDIR *directory specifier*

Directory specifier is the directory path name, with subdirectories separated by backslashes (\). The new directory will be created on the logged drive by default. If you omit the leading \ in your path, the new directory is added below your current directory. For example, assume that drive C is the logged disk drive. You want to add a directory called TEMP to hold temporary files. At the DOS prompt, enter

MKDIR \TEMP

Press the Enter key. DOS creates the TEMP directory directly under the root directory (\). You can use the DIR command to verify that the TEMP directory exists.

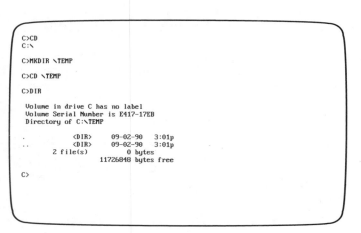

These commands show the name of the current directory, make a \TEMP directory, and display the new directory's contents.

```
C>CD
C:\

C>MKDIR \TEMP

C>CD \TEMP

C>DIR

 Volume in drive C has no label
 Volume Serial Number is E417-17EB
 Directory of C:\TEMP

.              <DIR>      09-02-90    3:01p
..             <DIR>      09-02-90    3:01p
     2 file(s)              0 bytes
                     11726848 bytes free

C>
```

CD shows the current directory. The current directory is the root directory (\). MD makes a new directory called TEMP. CD\TEMP changes current directory to TEMP. DIR displays contents of the TEMP directory.

To make a directory anywhere in the file system, use the MKDIR command with the full path name of the directory. The leading backslash shows the path from the root.

You can make a subdirectory of a subdirectory, as illustrated in the following diagram.

This directory structure shows how new directory branches are added to the hierarchical file-structure tree.

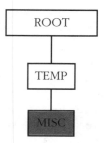

Note in the next screen that only the new directory name needs to be specified to create the MISC subdirectory below \TEMP. This is so because \TEMP is the current directory. The MISC subdirectory could have been created from anywhere within the file system by using the command MKDIR\TEMP\MISC.

122

```
C>CD \TEMP

C>CD
C:\TEMP

C>MD MISC

C>DIR

 Volume in drive C has no label
 Volume Serial Number is E417-17EB
 Directory of C:\TEMP

              <DIR>       09-07-90    3:44p
 ..           <DIR>       09-07-90    3:44p
 MISC         <DIR>       09-08-90   11:57a
      3 file(s)            0 bytes
                     11857920 bytes free

 C>
```

This screen shows that the current sub-directory is \TEMP. To create a subdirectory called MISC under \TEMP, issue the command, MKDIR MISC.

The CHDIR Command

Use the CHDIR or CD command to change to another directory or to display the path name of the current directory. Both CHDIR and CD work exactly alike. The CD command changes your position in the tree structure of directories. Decide which subdirectory you want as a working directory. Issue the command at the DOS prompt in the form

CD *directory specifier*

A directory specifier is the path name of the directory you want as the new current directory. Notice that the CD command has the same form as the MKDIR command. To change to the TEMP directory of the preceding example, enter the command

CD \TEMP

You can confirm that DOS changed your working directory to \TEMP. Just issue the CD command with no parameters, and DOS displays the current directory's path name. CD is an important command for DOS beginners. You can use CD to change to a directory from which you want information. Whenever you are positioned in the directory that holds the commands or data you need to use, you can omit the directory name from the command line. When you issue the CD command, the directory you change to becomes the default directory.

6

The RMDIR Command

You use the RMDIR or RD command to remove (delete) directories when you no longer need them. The command names RMDIR and RD work exactly alike. Before you remove a directory, the directory must be empty of all files and subdirectories. You cannot delete your current working directory.

The usual reason you get error messages when you use hierarchical directory commands is that you are not where you think you are in the hierarchical directory structure. The CD command lets you know where you are.

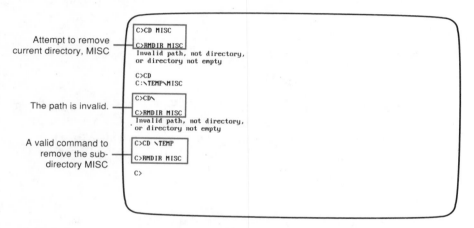

Attempt to remove current directory, MISC

The path is invalid.

A valid command to remove the sub-directory MISC

```
C>CD MISC

C>RMDIR MISC
Invalid path, not directory,
or directory not empty

C>CD
C:\TEMP\MISC

C>CD\

C>RMDIR MISC
Invalid path, not directory,
or directory not empty

C>CD \TEMP

C>RMDIR MISC

C>
```

RMDIR MISC command generates two error messages because of the way it is issued. The command RMDIR MISC, issued from the current directory, is invalid. You cannot remove the current directory.

In the second example, the current directory is the root. MISC is not a subdirectory of the root directory; therefore, DOS can not find the path to the MISC subdirectory from the root. The error here is an invalid path. This message also appears if a directory holds any files except the . and .. directories. You don't have to erase these files to remove a directory.

In the third command example, \TEMP is the current directory. From it, you can erase the empty subdirectory MISC.

If you want to delete your working directory, you must first change to another directory and delete all the files from the unwanted directory. For

124

RMDIR to work, the directory you change to must not contain the directory you want to delete as part of its path name. To remove a directory from the logged drive, issue the RMDIR command at the DOS prompt in the form

RMDIR *directory pathname*

To delete the TEMP directory used in the examples, you issue the command as follows:

RMDIR \TEMP

The PATH Command

If the file for the command you want DOS to execute is not in the current directory, you must give DOS the correct path.

The PATH command instructs DOS to use a certain route to find files. Most often, you use the PATH command to find an external DOS command. COMMAND.COM also uses the PATH command to find and start programs that are not in the current directory.

DOS knows how to find external command files in three situations:

1. The file is in the current directory in which you are working.

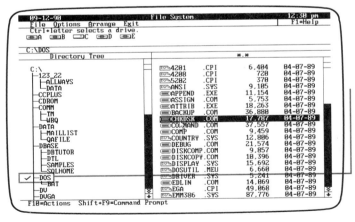

CHKDSK is in the current directory, \DOS.

2. The file is not in the current directory, but you include the full path on the command line: C:\DOS\CHKDSK A:

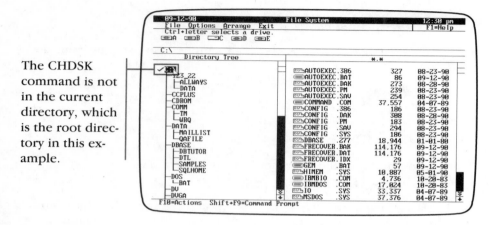

The CHDSK command is not in the current directory, which is the root directory in this example.

3. The directory in which the file is located is on the search path established by the PATH command. This PATH command instructs DOS to search each directory shown:

PATH=C:\DOS;C:\TEMP;C:\MISC;C:\LOTUS;C:\;

This directory structure shows the four subdirectories included in the preceding PATH statement.

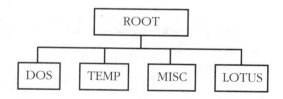

DOS retains the PATH until you change the command or reboot the computer. If you include more than one directory path in the command, you must separate the paths with a semicolon (;) character. To issue the PATH command for the logged drive, at the DOS prompt type

PATH *d:path specifier;d:path specifier;...*

The drive specifier *d:* names the drive on which DOS is to search. The first *path specifier* is the first directory on the search path. The semicolon (;) separates the first directory from the optional second. The ellipsis simply means that you can have other path specifiers in your command line.

If you create a \DOS directory to store the DOS utility files, You then include C:\DOS in the PATH command.

Once the PATH command is issued, whenever you use an external DOS command in a directory other than \DOS, the PATH specification leads COMMAND.COM to the command's program file in the \DOS directory.

The TREE Command

When you add many directories to your disk, you may lose track of the directory names and what files they contain. You can trace the organization of the directory with the TREE command.

6

TREE's output helps you see the framework of your disk's hierarchical structure.

You can use TREE to display all directory paths on the logged disk and, as an option, each directory's files. To list all directories, issue the TREE command at the DOS prompt in the form:

TREE \ /F

```
C:\>TREE B: /F
Directory PATH listing
Volume Serial Number is 2414-1EF7
B:.
├───DOS
│       SHELL.CLR
│       BACKUP.COM
│       CHKDSK.COM
│       COMMAND.COM
│       SHELLB.COM
│       BASICA.EXE
│       EXE2BIN.EXE
│       SHELLC.EXE
│       SHELL.HLP
│       SHELL.MEU
│
├───LOTUS
├───TEMP
│   └───MISC
│           MYFILE.MEM

C:\>
```

/F is an optional
switch. It tells
DOS to list the
file names in the
listing of directo-
ries.

If the output information is too much for one screen, you can stop the scrolling with the Ctrl-S key sequence. You restart the scrolling by pressing any key. You can get a printout of the results of the TREE command. Chapter 9 shows you how to redirect a command's output to your printer or to a file.

Lessons Learned

■ DOS organizes directories in a manner similar to the way a library breaks down books by subject subgroupings.

■ Although such terms as root and tree are established directory terminology, the directory concept is more like a foot path used for arriving at your destination.

■ The path concept is essentially the mapping out of a course for DOS to search.

■ The root directory is the beginning, or default, directory.

■ MD or MKDIR makes a directory.

■ CD or CHDIR changes from one directory to another.

■ RD or RMDIR removes a directory.

In Chapter 7, you'll learn how to become a copycat.

128

Copying, Erasing, and Renaming Files

7

Until the invention of the printing press, one of the most prestigious occupations was that of scribe. In cloistered solitude, the scribe devoted his life to copying books by hand. This effort saved many texts from oblivion because of neglect during the Dark Ages.

Almost certainly, scribes made mistakes, but they compensated for them by profusely illustrating each assigned book with gold leaf. Art has frequently been employed to hide cracks in walls. In this case, art played down the number of misplaced words and bad translations.

You have become a modern day scribe, with editing and copying speeds measured in milliseconds, rather than years. Your tools are the microcomputer, your fingers, and a few DOS commands.

In this chapter, you will learn how to copy the contents of one disk to another disk and compare them for accuracy, copy single or groups of files between disks, copy files with the same or different file names, erase or rename files in groups, and use the COPY command to enhance disk organization.

Key Terms Used in This Chapter

Source   The disk or file *from* which you are copying.

Destination   The disk or file *to* which you are copying.

Target   Same as destination.

Fragmentation   A condition that results when pieces of a disk file
                  are contained in sectors that are not contiguous—
                  or adjoining—because of adding and deleting files.
                  Fragmentation affects a hard disk's performance.

Current directory The directory that DOS uses as the default
                  directory. The root directory is the current
                  directory on the logged drive until you change to
                  another directory with the CHDIR (CD) command.

Overwrite   Writing new information over old in a disk file.

7

Files and Labels

Disk files are the primary storage place for data and programs. A knowledge
of how to manage these files is essential. If you want to be in control of your
work, you must be in control of your files. This chapter tells you how to copy
disks and files, erase unneeded files, and rename existing files.

When you work with floppy disks, always keep the labels on your disks
accurate. Use a felt-tipped pen and indicate the contents on the disk label as
you work. Disks not labeled or labeled wrong are an invitation to lost data. If
you do not label disks, you might mistake them for blank, unformatted disks.

Never use a ball point pen to write on a label that has been placed on a
floppy disk. The jacket doesn't keep the pen point from possibly damaging
the magnetic media and harming the disk.

130

Using DISKCOPY to Copy Disks

The DISKCOPY command makes an exact copy of another disk. DISKCOPY reads the input, or *source*, disk and then writes the data to another disk, the *destination* disk. DISKCOPY is good to use when you want to make a working copy of a master disk. You can then store the master disk in a safe place. DISKCOPY also copies the system files from a bootable source disk to make a copy that is bootable.

The basic DISKCOPY command assumes that your source and destination disks are the same size and capacity. You may find another Que title, *MS-DOS User's Guide*, Special Edition, helpful if you want more information on DISKCOPY.

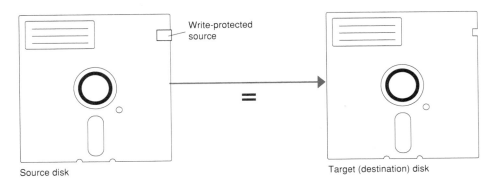

Write-protected source

Source disk   Target (destination) disk

The DISKCOPY command creates a duplicate of another disk. Both source and destination disks need to be the same size and capacity.

DISKCOPY is an external command. You must have the disk that contains DISKCOPY in your default drive or, if you have a hard disk, set the correct path with the PATH command (see Chapter 6). Use the DISKCOPY command to copy floppies only. The correct syntax for DISKCOPY is

   DISKCOPY *source d: destination d:*

Reading the syntax in the above description, some PC users could make a mistake. Another way to read it is

   DISKCOPY *source drive letter: destination drive letter:*

131

source drive letter is the name for the drive that holds the disk that you want to copy. *destination drive letter* is the name of the drive that holds the disk to receive the copy.

As always, type a colon after the drive name. Insert a space between the source and destination drive names. If you use a blank disk as the destination disk, DOS formats it with no instruction on your part. An example of the command is

DISKCOPY A: B:

After you use the DISKCOPY A: B: command, DOS prompts you to put the disks into the proper drives. Make sure that you put them in the correct drives. If you write-protect the source disk, its contents are safeguarded in case of a mix-up.

To write-protect a minifloppy disk, simply use a piece of tape to cover the little notch on the right side of the disk. These adhesive tabs usually come with a box of disks.

Strike a key, and the copy process begins. When the copy process finishes, DOS asks if you want to make another copy. Answer **Y** or **N**. You can make another copy now. If you answer Y, you do not have to access DISKCOPY again because DOS has the program in memory.

The common syntax for DISKCOPY is DISKCOPY A: B:. DOS prompts you to insert the diskettes before copying begins.

```
A>DISKCOPY A: B:

Insert SOURCE diskette in drive A:

Press any key to continue . . .

Copying 40 tracks
9 Sectors/Track, 2 Side(s)

Insert TARGET diskette in drive A:

Press any key to continue . . .

Volume Serial Number is 12D0-1261

Copy another diskette (Y/N)? N

A>
```

If you leave out the drive names in the DISKCOPY command line, DOS uses the default drive as the specifier. To avoid confusion, always type both the source and destination drive names after the DISKCOPY command.

Remember, you can only copy entire disks if both of the drives are compatible. For example, if your system contains two 360K floppy drives, DISKCOPY works fine. On the other hand, should one of your drives be a 1.2M floppy and the other a 360K floppy, you have to be more careful.

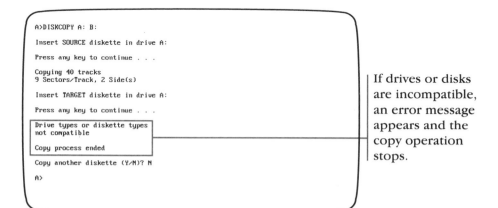

```
A>DISKCOPY A: B:

Insert SOURCE diskette in drive A:

Press any key to continue . . .

Copying 40 tracks
9 Sectors/Track, 2 Side(s)

Insert TARGET diskette in drive A:

Press any key to continue . . .

Drive types or diskette types
not compatible

Copy process ended

Copy another diskette (Y/N)? N

A>
```

If drives or disks are incompatible, an error message appears and the copy operation stops.

A 1.2M floppy disk drive can read 360K disks and thus makes an excellent source drive for DISKCOPY. Do not, however, attempt a DISKCOPY with a 360K disk as the source and a 1.2M drive as the destination.

If one of your drives is a 360K or 1.2M floppy, and the other is a 720K or 1.44M microfloppy drive, don't try to use DISKCOPY for disks of different capacities. Instead, you should format the destination disk first and then use the COPY command. We discuss this procedure in depth later.

If you have only one disk drive, the DISKCOPY process is still simple, if a bit more inconvenient. First, you type:

DISKCOPY A: A:

If your disk drive is 360K, everything is done in one operation, because your PC probably has more than 360K of RAM to hold the data. However, when

133

you use DISKCOPY with a 720K, 1.2M, or 1.44M drive, a prompt appears to tell you to swap disks until the operation is complete.

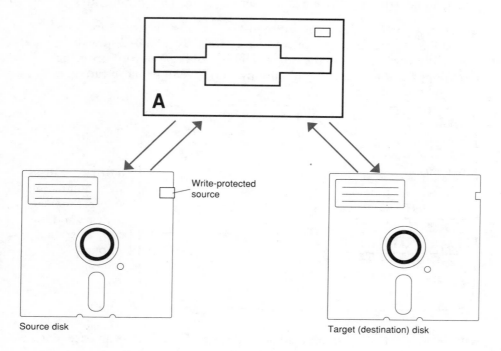

Source disk

Write-protected source

Target (destination) disk

Another word for those of you with two compatible disk drives: Remember, your source does not necessarily have to be drive A and the destination drive B. It can as easily be the reverse. But frankly, going from A to B—rather than from B to A—is easier, and you are less likely to make a mistake. If you have any doubts, try reciting the alphabet backwards.

Using DISKCOMP To Compare Disks

DOS is very good at making duplicates of disks. Most experienced people feel that using DISKCOMP is not normally necessary. However, you can confirm that two disks are identical by using the external DISKCOMP command.

DISKCOMP compares disks sector by sector. Remember that the disks and capacities must be the same for both disks in the comparison. Any difference in disks made with DISKCOPY is a sign of a problem disk. Issue the command in the form

DISKCOMP *source d: destination d:*

Load the two disks at the prompt, and DOS confirms the comparison or points out the differences. As with DISKCOPY, you can repeat the DISKCOMP command. An example of the DISKCOMP command is

DISKCOMP A: B:

If you omit a drive designator, DOS uses the default drive. When DISKCOMP is issued with no parameters, DOS will carry out the comparison using just one drive. DOS will alternately prompt you to switch between inserting the first and second disks. Depending on your system's memory, you will swap disks once or several times.

7

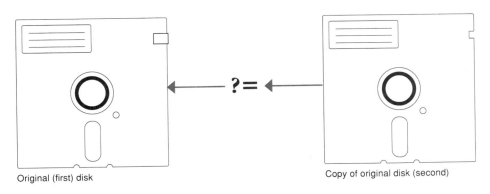

Original (first) disk   Copy of original disk (second)

The DISKCOMP command compares two disks of equal size and capacity to confirm that both are the same.

135

Normally, you use DISKCOMP to test disks originally made with the DISKCOPY command. If the disks compare, DOS gives the message Compare OK.

In the following example, a defective working copy of a master disk is compared to the master. Notice the compare error.

The working copy is no longer identical to the master. To solve the problem, make a new working copy.

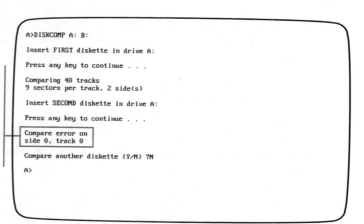

```
A>DISKCOMP A: B:

Insert FIRST diskette in drive A:

Press any key to continue . . .

Comparing 40 tracks
9 sectors per track, 2 side(s)

Insert SECOND diskette in drive A:

Press any key to continue . . .

Compare error on
side 0, track 0

Compare another diskette (Y/N) ?N

A>
```

7

Mastering the COPY Command

The internal COPY command is a DOS workhorse. It is probably one of the five most frequently issued DOS commands and should be fully understood. COPY, RENAME and DELETE are powerful tools that can give you a confident feeling of complete control.

However, you should not use these three commands if your mind is preoccupied with matters unrelated to your PC. Take a nap, watch TV, or drink coffee first. These commands are DOS power tools and should only be used by those who are alert and careful.

The DISKCOPY command works with disks; the COPY command handles files. Because COPY is an internal command, you can issue it at any time at the DOS prompt. You can use COPY to move files between disks of different sizes and capacities.

COPY is a versatile command that allows wild cards in the syntax. In this book, you will learn how to use the COPY command as you most likely would in daily computing.

Understanding the Principles of COPY

The COPY command has many variations, yet every COPY command copies data from a source to a destination. DOS uses the following items in the example to determine the source and destination.

The names of disk drives:

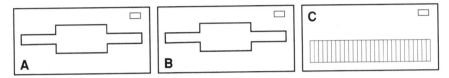

The names of path(s), if any:

The file name and extension:

This is an example of copying a file from a source to a destination:

In the full form of COPY, the drive, the path, and the file name and extension are given for both the source and destination file. The full form of COPY can

137

be used for every COPY command if you want. However, if either the source or destination path is the current path, you can omit the path name.

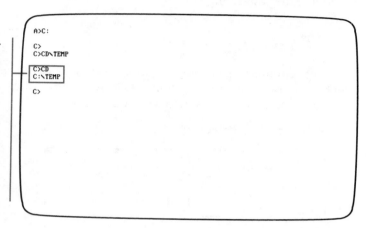

To make a directory current, issue the CD command with the directory's name. The CD command with no parameters shows the current directory path.

You can use wild cards (? and *) in the file name and extension to allow the COPY command to match source files and copy them to destination files. The power of copying multiple files with wild cards is a good reason to choose file names that lend themselves to matching with wild cards.

If the destination file name is omitted, DOS uses the source file name as the name for the new, copied file.

```
C:\TEMP>COPY *.DOC B:\
17THCENT.DOC
17THFINL.DOC
ADAM_EVE.DOC
        3 File(s) copied

C:\TEMP>
```

Using the Full Form of COPY

When you first begin to copy files, you may be most comfortable using the full syntax of the COPY command. This "safety net" method requires more keystrokes, but it pays off in trouble-free file manipulation. As you gain experience, however, you may want to refer to some of the variations shown on the following pages.

The syntax of the COPY command is

> **COPY *sd:\path\filename.ext dd:\path\filename.ext/V***

The ***sd:*** is the name of the source file's drive and ***dd:*** is the name of the destination file's drive. The ***\path\filename.ext*** is the full path name for the file in the directory tree structure. The ***/V*** is an optional switch that tells DOS to verify that a copy is exact. A delimiting space separates the source and destination parts of the command. An example of the full COPY command is

> COPY C:\MISC\MYFILE.MEM A:\KEEP\MYFILE.KEP/V

MYFILE.MEM is a file located on drive C in the \MISC directory. You want to copy the file to a new file named MYFILE.KEP in the \KEEP directory on drive A. Because of default values in this example, you might omit some of the items of syntax without disturbing the copying process.

The following illustration shows how the full COPY command gives DOS the parameters needed to find a file on the directory tree of the source disk and creates the new file name on the destination disk. These parameters also tell DOS to verify that the copied file is an exact duplicate. The full version of the COPY command does not rely on DOS's current default drive or directory.

7

Command as issued:

COPY C:\MISC\MYFILE.MEM A:\KEEP\MYFILE.KEP/V

What DOS knows by the rule of currents:

Every parameter that DOS needs is supplied in this full version of the command.

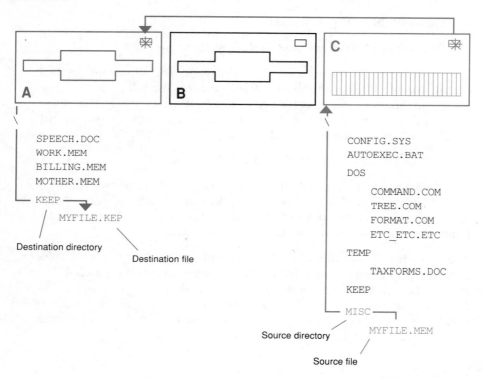

```
                    A                        B                        C
SPEECH.DOC                                          CONFIG.SYS
WORK.MEM                                            AUTOEXEC.BAT
BILLING.MEM                                         DOS
MOTHER.MEM                                              COMMAND.COM
KEEP                                                    TREE.COM
     MYFILE.KEP                                         FORMAT.COM
                                                        ETC_ETC.ETC
Destination directory                               TEMP
          Destination file                              TAXFORMS.DOC
                                                    KEEP
                                                    MISC
                                                        MYFILE.MEM
                                        Source directory
                                                Source file
```

The slash (/) and backslash (\) characters are both typed with the right fingers. While dashing off a command or two, it is probable you will sooner or later substitute one for the other. Just remember that the backslash is the key on the upper right corner of your board. It indicates the path to wherever you wish to go or reference. The slash is the key on the lower right hand corner of your keyboard. This slash is used for optional switches.

Everyone presses the wrong keys from time to time, so it is good policy to use care when adding slashes. In fact, issuing commands is definitely not the place to improve your touch-typing skills.

Using COPY To Handle Defaults

You learned about default values in earlier chapters, but you also need to know how DOS handles defaults in COPY commands. The *rule of currents* states that if you do not specify a drive in the copy command, DOS uses the current (default or logged) drive.

If you do not specify a path in the command, DOS uses the current directory of the disk. If you do not specify a destination file name, the copied file keeps the same file name as the source file. You will see how the rule of currents applies to COPY in later examples.

If you give a disk drive letter and path for the source file, but omit the file name, DOS assumes that you want to copy every file in the directory. This assumption is comparable to using the wild card *.* as the file specifier for the source file.

COPY is a dangerous command because it overwrites on the destination disk files whose names duplicate file names on the source disk. Always check directories for duplicate file names before you try copying files. It is also easy to confuse disk drives. You can easily copy old versions over new file versions. Using wild cards as part of file names during the COPY process also can produce unexpected results. Remember, COPY does what you instruct it to do. Make sure that you do not tell COPY to do something you don't want it to do.

If you are unsure about COPY command syntax, write-protect your source disk if it is a floppy.

Whether or not it appears necessary, many experienced computer users protect themselves by adding drive specifications whenever they issue a DOS command. Including drive letters as a "safety net" can save a good deal of grief.

Copying All Files in a Directory

One reason for using the COPY command is to increase the efficiency of disk operations in your computer. As you add and delete files from a disk, the

141

free space for new file information becomes physically spread around the surface of the disk. This phenomenon is called *fragmentation* and proves that even technological marvels can be sloppy housekeepers.

DOS allocates data storage space by finding the next available disk space. If the first available space is too small to hold an entire file, DOS fills that space and puts the rest of the file into the next available space(s). Fragmented files lower disk performance.

If you use DISKCOPY on a fragmented floppy disk, you get an exact image of the fragmented disk. To avoid copying fragmentation, or to make an efficient copy of a fragmented floppy disk, use the COPY command. First, be sure that the destination disk is formatted and make sure that the disk contains enough room to hold the source file(s). The source files are then copied, with no fragmentation, to the destination disk. Simply place the source disk in drive A and the destination disk in drive B and type:

   COPY A:*.* B:

In this example, you copied all files on the disk in drive A to the disk in drive B and kept the same file names. (Remember the rule of currents.) By changing to a directory on your hard disk, you can copy all files from the disk in drive B to your hard disk:

   COPY B:*.* C:

Copying Files between Disks

You can copy one file or many files to another disk for backing up a disk, moving data to another computer, or any other purpose. The following example copies files between floppy disks. The steps are logical when laid out one at a time:

1. Use the COPY command with a file name or a wild card that matches the file(s) you want to move to the other disk.
2. Put the disk with the source file(s) in drive A.
3. Put the destination disk in drive B.
4. Type **DIR A:** to see the size of the file(s) you want to copy.
5. Type **DIR B:** to see if the destination disk contains sufficient free space.

6. If sufficient space is on the destination disk, enter the COPY command. An example of this command is

   COPY A:*.MEM B:/V

Here, DOS copies all files with the extension MEM to the disk in drive B and verifies the copy. The /V switch is optional and almost doubles the time for making a copy. However, it is worthwhile to make sure that the copies are perfect. The destination file name was omitted here. DOS accepts the original names by default unless you specify otherwise.

You can omit the name of your logged drive (A:) from this example, but to be safe, you should include it. This procedure adds the "safety belt" mentioned earlier.

Command as issued:

   COPY A:*.MEM B:

What DOS knows by the rule of currents:

   COPY A:*.MEM B:*.MEM

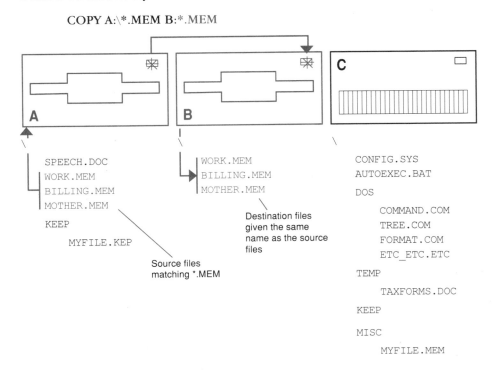

```
                                          \                    CONFIG.SYS
       SPEECH.DOC            WORK.MEM                           AUTOEXEC.BAT
       WORK.MEM             BILLING.MEM                         DOS
       BILLING.MEM          MOTHER.MEM
       MOTHER.MEM                                                   COMMAND.COM
                                                                    TREE.COM
       KEEP                                                         FORMAT.COM
                                                                    ETC_ETC.ETC
           MYFILE.KEP                                          TEMP

                                                                   TAXFORMS.DOC

                                                               KEEP

                                                               MISC

                                                                   MYFILE.MEM
```

Destination files given the same name as the source files

Source files matching *.MEM

143

Copying a Single File from One Disk to Another

The following example of the COPY command copies a single file from one disk to another. The root directories of the two disks are current and can be omitted from the command. Since the destination file name is omitted, the copied file will have the same name and extension as the source file. The /V switch verifies the copy.

Command as issued:

COPY A:SPEECH.DOC B:/V

What DOS knows by the rule of currents:

COPY A:\SPEECH.DOC B:\SPEECH.DOC /V

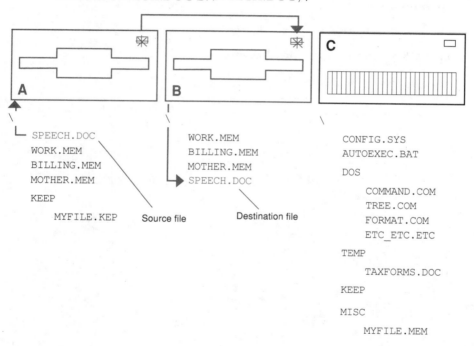

This command copies the SPEECH.DOC file from the disk in drive A to the disk in drive B. The root directories of the two disks are the current directories and can be omitted from the command. Since the destination file name is omitted, the copied file have the same name and extension as the source file. The /V switch verifies the copy.

144

Copying from a Floppy Disk to a Hard Disk

If you have a hard disk, you can use the COPY command as in the following example to copy a file from a floppy disk to a hard disk. In this example, the directory \KEEP was made current on drive C with a CD \KEEP command. The path specifiers for the source and destination drives are omitted. The /V switch verifies the copy. This form of COPY is good for preserving a copy of a file in case the original file is erased or rendered incorrect.

Command as issued:

COPY A:SPEECH.DOC C:/V

What DOS knows by the rule of currents:

COPY A:\SPEECH.DOC C:\KEEP\SPEECH.DOC /V

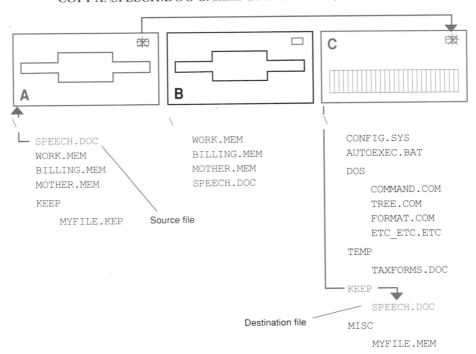

This command line copies the SPEECH file from the floppy disk in drive A to the current directory of the hard disk.

Copying a File to the Same Disk Directory

Occasionally, you need to create a duplicate of a file on the same disk and in the same directory. (For this example, assume that floppy disks have only one directory, the root.) DOS does not allow duplicate file names and extensions in the same directory. You must give a file another name, another extension, or both if you want a duplicate. Most people give the file a different extension and keep the file name the same.

To duplicate a file and place it in the same directory, you must enter a source file name and a destination file name in the command line. The following example illustrates this rule.

Command as issued:

COPY SPEECH.DOC SPEECH.BAK

What DOS knows by the rule of currents:

COPY C:\KEEP\SPEECH.DOC C:\KEEP\SPEECH.BAK

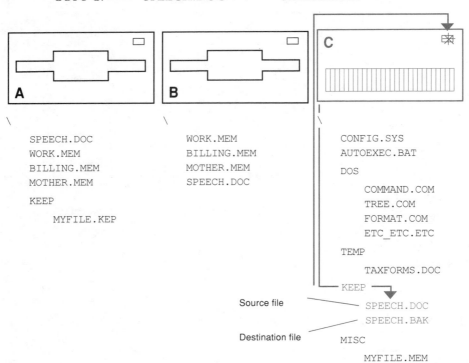

In this example, you used the rule of currents. Because you did not specify a drive, DOS used the default drive. You now have a copy of SPEECH.DOC named SPEECH.BAK. By using the BAK extension, you can recognize the new file as a backup of the original file. You also might give the destination file a completely new name. In this example, you can get a directory listing of both files with the following command:

DIR SPEECH.*

After the copy, the two files contain the same information (as with any copy). This form of COPY is good for preserving a copy of a file in case the original file is erased or rendered incorrect.

Copying a File across Directories

If you have a hard disk, you need a method of copying files from one directory to another. For this use of COPY, assume that you are already in the directory that contains the source files(s) and that you have created the destination directory. Although this discussion of COPY can apply to floppy disks that have subdirectories, users of hard disks are more likely to encounter this situation.

You can have duplicate file names and extensions in *different* directories if you like. Therefore, you can omit the destination file names for this example. Because your current directory is the one containing the source file, you can omit the source path.

7

147

Command as issued:

COPY SPEECH.DOC \MISC /V

What DOS knows by the rule of currents:

COPY C:\KEEP\ SPEECH.DOC C: \MISC\SPEECH.DOC /V

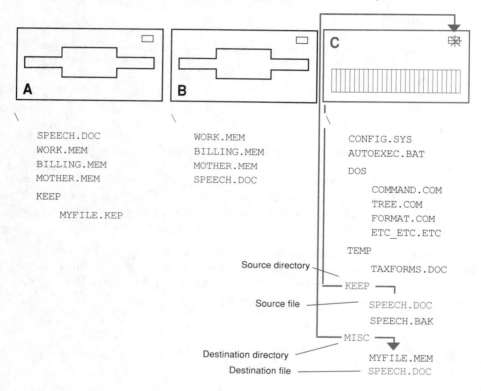

This command copies the file SPEECH.DOC from the current drive and directory. You now have a copy of SPEECH.DOC in the subdirectory \MISC on the current drive. The command also verifies the copy.

When you copy files between subdirectories, the DOS CD command is useful. Using the CD command with a directory name changes the default directory. You can verify your location by using the CD command with no parameters. Use CD to change the current directory to the source file's directory. You can then take advantage of the rule of currents by omitting the source file's drive and path names in the command.

Copying Safety versus Speed

Let's quickly review three key ways of issuing key commands:

COPY SPEECH.DOC A:

> The fastest method of typing the command and copying file(s). However, it offers the least guarantee of an accurate copy and, although errors are unlikely, they can occur.

COPY C:SPEECH.DOC A:

> Identifies the default drive (C:), double-checking your own actions.

COPY C:SPEECH.DOC A:/V

> The /V switch verifies an accurate copy; accounts for both human and mechanical fallibility.

Whether or not you use safety measures is your decision. However, it is wise to begin a relationship with DOS on a conservative note. Remember, a "safety belt" takes adding only the current drive letter and the /V.

Deleting and Renaming Files

When you no longer need a file, use the ERASE or DEL command to remove it from the disk. Erasing old work that is no longer of use is good computer housekeeping. The amount of free space on disks, especially hard disks, gets scarce if you do not erase unneeded files.

You can use the RENAME command to choose a better name for a file. If you use a program that overwrites your data file each time the program runs, you can save the file by renaming it. This method lets you keep both the new file and the original, renamed file.

Using ERASE or DEL

The internal commands ERASE or DEL work exactly alike. Both commands delete files. ERASE is easier to remember, but DEL is quicker to type. These commands are hazardous: make sure that you issue them correctly. Use extreme caution when you use wild cards with the ERASE command!

7

149

The syntax is

ERASE *path**filename*

or

DEL *path**filename*

The safest way to use the ERASE command is to change to the drive and directory that holds the file(s) you want to delete. You can use wild cards in the file name, but check the current file directory for other file names that might match the wild card you plan to use. You may not want to delete all files that match the wild card.

For example, with the current drive and directory as default you can type:

ERASE SPEECH.DOC

or

DEL SPEECH.DOC

to remove the file SPEECH.DOC.

7

If you use wild cards in the command, you can erase several files at one time. DOS issues an `Are you sure?` confirmation prompt if you use the wild card *.*. In all other cases, DOS is silent while deleting files. *Caution: if you omit the file-name specifier, but include a path specifier, DOS assumes that you want to use the *.* wild card.*

DOS carries out the ERASE command when you press Enter. If you make a mistake, the Ctrl-C or Ctrl-Break key sequence may stop the ERASE command in time to minimize the damage to your files.

The ERASE *filename* command deletes a file. To check to see whether the file was deleted, use the DIR command.

```
Volume in drive A has no label
Volume Serial Number is 201A-07C8
Directory of  A:\

SPEECH   DOC        80 09-07-90   3:54p
WORK     MEM        80 09-07-90   3:54p
MOTHER   MEM        80 09-07-90   3:54p
BILLING  MEM        80 09-07-90   3:55p
         4 File(s)       358400 bytes free

A>ERASE WORK.MEM

A>DIR

Volume in drive A has no label
Volume Serial Number is 201A-07C8
Directory of  A:\

SPEECH   DOC        80 09-07-90   3:54p
MOTHER   MEM        80 09-07-90   3:54p
BILLING  MEM        80 09-07-90   3:55p
         3 File(s)       359424 bytes free

A>
```

Use extreme care when you erase files. Exercise even more caution when you use wild cards to erase files.

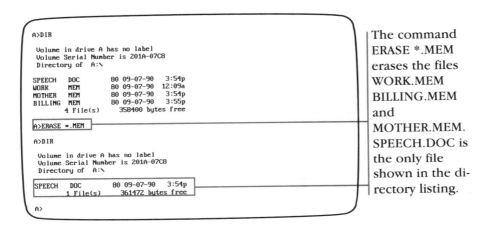

The command ERASE *.MEM erases the files WORK.MEM BILLING.MEM and MOTHER.MEM. SPEECH.DOC is the only file shown in the directory listing.

Using RENAME

When you name a file, the name you choose is not permanent. You can use the RENAME (abbreviated REN) command to rename a file. The commands work exactly alike, but RENAME is probably easier to remember.

The syntax for RENAME is

RENAME *d:path\filename.ext filename.ext*

You can use RENAME to change either the file name or the extension, or both. DOS assumes that a wild card (*) in the destination file name or extension means "use the original name." Using wild cards in the source file name or extension can have unexpected results in the renaming process.

As a precaution, use the DIR command with the proposed wild card to see which files are affected. Again, change to the disk and directory that contains the file(s) to exploit DOS's defaults. You issue a command like:

RENAME SPEECH.BAK SPEECH.DOC

151

Remember that you cannot duplicate a file name in the same directory. If a name conflict arises, rename or erase the file with the conflicting name and then issue the RENAME command.

RENAME is a valuable disk-maintenance command. The directory listing shows that the file SPEECH.DOC is now named SPEECH.BAK.

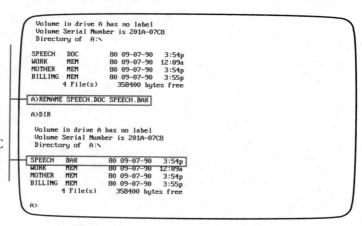

```
Volume in drive A has no label
Volume Serial Number is 201A-07C8
Directory of  A:\

SPEECH   DOC        80 09-07-90   3:54p
WORK     MEM        80 09-07-90  12:09a
MOTHER   MEM        80 09-07-90   3:54p
BILLING  MEM        80 09-07-90   3:55p
         4 File(s)       358400 bytes free

A>RENAME SPEECH.DOC SPEECH.BAK

A>DIR

Volume in drive A has no label
Volume Serial Number is 201A-07C8
Directory of  A:\

SPEECH   BAK        80 09-07-90   3:54p
WORK     MEM        80 09-07-90  12:09a
MOTHER   MEM        80 09-07-90   3:54p
BILLING  MEM        80 09-07-90   3:55p
         4 File(s)       358400 bytes free

A>
```

7 Lessons Learned

- The computer revolution allows text to be copied more quickly and more accurately than at any other time in history.
- DISKCOPY makes an exact copy of a disk.
- DISKCOMP insures that data has been copied with absolute precision.
- The COPY command copies single or multiple files on one disk or from one disk to another.
- The COPY command also places a copy of a file into any directory you want.
- The DEL or ERASE command deletes one or more files.
- The REN or RENAME command renames one or more files.

Now and then, to keep your healthy computer healthy demands preventive medicine. That topic is taken up in Chapter 8.

Practicing Preventive Medicine with Your PC

8

Surely you have waited by the TV or radio, expecting an optimistic weather report. This is particularly true in the summer. It is during the warm season that forecasters unfailingly joke, "It's not the heat, it's the humidity." Of course, this comment implies that humidity, not the temperature, makes you uncomfortable.

Perhaps so. Humidity affects some people more than others, and the same is true of computers. For example, even with today's advances, large computer systems demand constant temperature and humidity control. Fortunately, the PC is more resilient than its big brother. A good rule is that if you are uncomfortable, your computer probably is too. Extremes in temperature affect hardware performance, including your computer's ability to "think."

> ## Key Terms Used in This Chapter
>
> **Surge suppressor** A protective device inserted between a power outlet and a computer's power plug. Surge suppressors help block power surges that often damage computer circuits.
>
> **Static electricity** A charge that builds on an object and that can be discharged when another object is touched. Electronic circuits are easily damaged by static electricity discharges.
>
> **Ground** An electrical path directly to the center prong of an outlet. Grounds can safely dissipate static discharges.
>
> **Voltage regulator** An electrical device that keeps voltage fluctuations from reaching an electrical device. Regulators usually don't stop power surges.

8

Also, remember Murphy's Law. If something can go wrong, it will. When you least expect—or can afford—it, disaster strikes. The disaster can sneak up on you as computer malfunction, disk aging, or inconsistent electrical current. A chance exists that, sooner or later, you will lose important data.

And then there is human error. For example, you may be inclined to issue ill-timed DELETE or COPY commands. It's a human trait to get a little careless when you are tired or excited.

The information presented in this chapter might save your invaluable data. This chapter also will help keep Murphy's Law at bay by preventing hardware and software failures. You will learn that proper use of the BACKUP and RESTORE commands can reduce the risk of losing valuable data.

Avoiding Data Loss

As you use your computer, you will create a multitude of files. Many of these files contain precious information. Because of the reliable nature of today's computers, you may be tempted to trust that these files will "be there when you need them." However, as an old computer saying goes, "There are two kinds of computer users: those who have lost files, and those who are going to lose files."

You can start by protecting your files from real-world menaces. Some of these are humidity, static discharge, excessive heat, and erratic electrical power.

The most important data-protection measure you can take is learning to make backup copies of your disk files. Although DISKCOPY and COPY are adequate for creating safety copies of floppy disks, hard disk files are often too big to fit on a floppy disk. And yet, just one errant wild-card ERASE command can delete dozens of files from a hard disk in seconds.

This chapter covers basic BACKUP and RESTORE command techniques. With the examples in this chapter, you will learn to back up and restore your entire hard disk. You also will learn the various switches to use to adapt BACKUP and RESTORE for your particular needs.

The BACKUP and RESTORE commands are effective insurance against file loss. You can insure against the loss of hours—or weeks—of work through methodical use of the BACKUP command to make backup disks of your files. Of course, you also should master the complement to BACKUP, the RESTORE command. RESTORE takes your backup disks and replaces files lost from your hard disk.

Many software houses have devised stand-alone backup software packages. These packages are quicker to learn and easier to control than the utilities in the DOS utilities package. In time, you may purchase one of these packages and scoff at BACKUP and RESTORE. Nevertheless, until you do, you should understand these important DOS utilities.

In theory, all backup software serves the same purpose. If you understand the benefits and the dangers native to each command and in each package, you can reliably use these utilities.

If you have not yet tried to back up disk files, or if you are learning your way around DOS, this chapter is important. If you apply this information, you may never experience the shock that comes to those who lose files.

Preventing Hardware Failures

Today's personal computers are reliable and economical data-processing machines. The latest generation of PCs do the work of mainframe computers that, a decade ago, only a fortunate few could access. However, as is true of any machine, computers break down and computer operators make mistakes.

Computers contain thousands of transistorized circuits. Under ideal conditions, most of these circuits can last a century or more. However, a poor power source, excessive heat, and static discharge can cripple these circuits until they grow erratic or fail.

Disk drives incorporate precise moving parts with critical alignments. The potential always exists for hardware failure. By following the precautions presented in this section, you reduce the odds of losing time and information because of hardware or software failure.

Always be vigilant about your computer's environment. A power strip with a built-in surge protector is a good start. If your power flutters and lights flicker, you probably need a line voltage regulator. Make sure that no electrical appliances near your computer pollute your power source. Connect your computer equipment to power sources not shared by copiers, TVs, fans, or other noise-generating electrical equipment.

Power strips keep your cables neat and rid your work area of strings of extension cords. Power surge suppressors are built into many power strips.

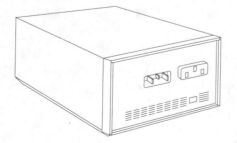

Line voltage regulators remove "dips" and "spikes" in electric power lines caused either by motors turning on or by other power reducers.

8

156

Is the fan on the back of your computer choked with dust? Clean the air vents and check that your computer has room to breathe. Your computer can become erratic when the temperature climbs. Circuits are not reliable when they overheat, and the condition can cause jumbled data. To make sure that your computer can breathe, keep it cool.

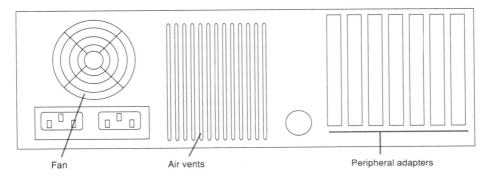

Fan   Air vents   Peripheral adapters

Use a soft blind-cleaner attachment on your vacuum cleaner to remove the dust build-up from your computer's breathing system.

Your body generates *static electricity* when humidity is low, when you wear synthetic fabrics, or when you walk across carpet. Just touching the keyboard while carrying a static charge can send an electrical shudder through your computer. This can cause data loss or circuit failure. Fortunately, you can avoid static problems by touching your grounded system unit's cabinet before touching the keyboard. If static electricity is a serious problem for you, ask your dealer about anti-static products.

Preventing Software Failures

Each software program you buy is a set of instructions for the microprocessor. A small minority of software packages have flawed instructions called *bugs*. Software bugs are usually minor and rarely cause more than keyboard lock-ups or jumbled displays. There is a possibility that these errors will cause your disk drive to operate in an erratic way, however. Fortunately, most firms test and debug their software before releasing the packages. Performing a backup of your software disks is good insurance against bugs.

Stopping small hardware or software problems before they become big ones takes a little planning and forethought. Table 8.1 lists a few simple yet successful "preventive solutions."

Table 8.1
Hardware and Software Problems and Remedies

Problem	Remedy
Static electricity	Anti-static liquid
	Anti-static floor mat
	"Touch Pad" on desk
Overheating	Clean clogged air vents
	Remove objects blocking vents
	Use air-conditioned room in summer
Damaged disks	Don't leave disks to be warped by sun
	Use protective covers
	Avoid spilling liquids on disks
	Store disks in a safe place
	Avoid magnetic fields from appliances (TVs, microwave ovens, etc.)
Software bugs	Buy tested commercial products

Preventing Your Mistakes

As you gain skill, you'll use DOS commands that can easily result in the unplanned loss of files. Commands such as COPY, ERASE, and FORMAT perform their jobs as you command. DOS does not know when a technically correct command will produce an unwanted effect. For this reason, always study what you type on the command line before you press Enter. It is too easy to develop a typing rhythm that speeds you through confirmation prompts into ruin. Remember, use Ctrl-C, Ctrl-Break, or—if necessary—Ctrl-Alt-Del to abandon commands. Because you are certain to make mistakes, always keep a recent backup copy of important data files.

Preparing for the Backup

DOS or your computer may have several different methods available to back up your files. For example, your computer could have a tape backup unit as part of its peripheral hardware. The methods for backing up files to tape also vary. You should know how to create and manipulate disk-based backups, however, in case you need to restore files to a computer that is not equipped with a tape backup.

With a single BACKUP command, you can back up an entire fixed disk. You also can use switches and parameters to make partial backups of the disk, backing up selected files only. You can select files by time, date, directory, activity, or file name.

Full Backup Considerations

A full backup makes backup copies of all files on the hard disk. BACKUP even copies hidden files. A full backup transfers the complete contents of your fixed disk onto backup disks.

How Often To Back Up Hard Disks

Performing a complete backup about once a month is a good habit. If you do not regularly schedule partial backups to copy your most important files, do a complete backup more often.

On any day, ask yourself, "If my hard drive failed today, how much data would I lose?" It is easier to perform a backup than to try to reconstruct lost data. DOS does not prompt you to make backups. The decision is yours. Let your conscience guide you. Remember, it's your data.

Preparing Backup Floppies

Before you perform a complete backup, make sure that you have enough floppy disks to hold all of the files that reside on your hard disk. You don't want to stop halfway through a backup to run to the computer store to buy more disks! DOS versions 3.3 and 4.XX are more efficient than older versions

8

159

in using backup space. The following formula calculates the approximate space you need for an entire backup:

1. Change to drive C.
2. Type **CD ** and press Enter.
3. Type **DIR** and press Enter.
4. Take the number of free bytes the directory displays and divide the number by 1,000,000. The remainder gives you a ballpark figure of the number of megabytes left on the disk.
5. Subtract the number of megabytes from the disk's total capacity.

You now have the approximate number of megabytes needed to calculate the backup. When you know the approximate number of megabytes, you can use table 8.2 to estimate the number of disks you need. If you run out of disks, you can stop the backup by pressing Ctrl-C.

Table 8.2
Floppy Disks Needed for Backup

Megabytes Used	Disk Capacity			
	360K	*720K*	*1.2M*	*1.44M*
10M	29	15	9	8
20M	59	29	18	15
30M	83	44	27	22
40M	116	58	35	29
70M	200	100	60	50

One drawback to backing up a hard disk is the time it takes. The hours, days, and—often—weeks of work you may one day save makes that time properly spent. Format the disks and number them consecutively. BACKUP copies disks in sequential order so that RESTORE can put back the files on your hard disk in the proper order. Do not use the /S switch when you format the disks. The /S switch decreases the available space on floppy disks.

You can use older disks that contain files you don't want to keep. BACKUP overwrites old files. When you finish the backup, arrange the disks numerically. Store them in a convenient part of your work space where they can stay in sequence.

If you have DOS V3.3, you can skip the formatting step. Simply include a /F (format) switch when you issue the BACKUP command. DOS V4.XX detects unformatted disks and formats them. The process takes longer to execute when BACKUP handles the formatting for you.

JANUARY						
1	2	3	4	5	6	7
8	9	10	11	12	13	14
15	16	BACK UP	18	19	20	21
22	23	24	25	26	27	28
29	30	31				

Try to pick a time at some regular interval to do a backup. Back up once per month or more often if you frequently change many files.

Get into the habit of performing a backup at least once a month. Mark the date on the calendar as a memory jogger.

Follow these steps to back up your hard disk:

1. Estimate how full your hard disk is.
2. Determine how many floppy disks you need for a backup (see table 8.2).
3. Format the floppies or use BACKUP /F if you have DOS V3.3 or later.

Remember that BACKUP is half of a useful pair of commands. The other half, RESTORE, retrieves files copied with BACKUP.

Issuing the BACKUP and RESTORE Commands

The BACKUP command can selectively copy files from your hard disk to the destination floppy disk. The internal format of the backed up file on the floppy is different from normal files. Therefore, you cannot use COPY to retrieve files stored on a backup disk.

8

The RESTORE command takes the files from your backup disks and copies them on your hard disk. Your computer may have a tape backup unit as part of its peripheral hardware.

Syntax for BACKUP

Your computer can use the files produced by BACKUP only after you run them through the RESTORE program. BACKUP is an external command. Include its path in the command line, or make sure that the command file is in the directory where the BACKUP command resides.

The symbolic syntax for BACKUP is

> **BACKUP *sd:spath\sfilename.ext dd: /switches***

The *sd:* represents the letter of the drive containing the source disk. This drive is usually drive C.

The *spath* symbolizes the path to the files for which you want to make backup copies.

The *sfilename.ext* notation is the full file name of the file(s) you want to back up. Full file names may contain wild cards for selective backup of matching files.

The *dd:* notation refers to the drive that receives the backup files.

The */switches* are optional switches that modify the basic BACKUP command. Not all switches are available in all versions of DOS. The DOS defaults also may vary from version to version.

Full Backup

The full backup puts all files on your backup floppies. The full backup requires about one minute for each floppy disk to be used in the backup. To do a full backup, change to the root directory and enter the following command:

> **BACKUP C:*.* A: /S**

This command tells DOS to back up all files in the root directory and to include all subdirectories (/S switch). DOS prompts you to insert and change disks.

Always put the backup date on the disks for future reference. Put the backup disks in the proper sequence and store the disks in a safe place.

Selective Backups

By specifying source directory paths, wild card file names or extensions, and switches, you can select specific files to back up. Selective backups are useful when just some of your data changes between full backups or if you move specific files from one computer system to another.

Specifying Selected Directory and File Names

BACKUP always starts in the directory you specify in the source path. If you place a directory name in the path at a point in the tree other than the root directory, you can back up files in that directory (and its subdirectories) with /S.

You can add further selectivity by using wild cards in the file name. For example, using a wild card for the root file name, as in *.DOC, selects all files that have the extension DOC.

Adding Other Backup Switches

The /M switch selects only those files that have changed since the last backup. The /D and /T switches select files based on date and, in versions 3.3 and 4.XX, on the time. Use the /D and /T switches when you want to select files based on a specific date or time.

You enter a date and, optionally, a time after the appropriate switch, using the same formats you use for the DATE and TIME commands. Files changed on or after a specified date and time are included in the backup. The /A switch adds files to a backup disk series and leaves the existing backup files intact. The /F switch formats the destination floppy as part of the BACKUP procedure in DOS V3.3. If necessary, DOS V4.XX automatically formats the floppy.

Table 8.3 lists examples of using switches with the BACKUP and RESTORE commands.

8

Table 8.3
BACKUP and RESTORE Switches

Switch	Description
BACKUP	
/M	Selects files whose contents have changed since the last BACKUP command backed them up.
/D	Selects files based on the date.
/T	Selects files based on the time (V3.3 and 4.XX).
/A	Adds new files to a backup disk series, but leaves the existing backup files intact.
/F	Formats the destination floppy as part of the BACKUP procedure in V3.3. If needed, V4.XX automatically formats the floppy.
RESTORE	
/P	Prompts the user if the file should be restored if it is marked as read-only or has been changed since the last backup.
/N	Restores only files that are no longer on the hard disk. This switch is useful if you accidentally deleted hard disk files and need to restore them from backups (new in DOS 3.3).
/M	Performs like /N but also restores files that have changed since the backup (new in DOS 3.3).
/B:date	Restores all files created or changed on or before the date.
/A:date	Restores all files created or changed on or after the specified date. This switch uses the DATE command format.
/E:time	Restores all files modified at or earlier than the specified time. This switch uses the TIME command format.
/L:time	Restores all files modified at or later than the specified time.

Syntax for RESTORE

The partner command to BACKUP is the DOS external command RESTORE. RESTORE is the only command that copies backed-up files to the hard disk. RESTORE's syntax is similar to BACKUP's syntax. Seen symbolically, the syntax is

RESTORE *sd: dd:\dpath\dfilename.ext /switches*

sd: refers to the source drive, that is, the name of the drive holding the files you want to restore.

The *dd:* is the hard disk you want to restore to (usually drive C).

The *dpath* notation represents the directory on the hard disk that receives the restored files. Files on the backup floppies that didn't come from the *dpath* are not restored.

The *dfilename.ext* is the file name for the file(s) to be restored. You can use wild cards in the file name to select specific files.

/switches stands for the optional switches you can add to gain further selectivity with the RESTORE command.

Restoring One File

You can choose to restore a single file by using a complete path and file name in the command. As in all selective restores, DOS prompts you to insert sequential disks until it locates the specified file.

Suppose that you want to restore the file \KEEP\SPEECH.DOC from the backup disk. The proper command is

RESTORE A: C:\KEEP\SPEECH.DOC

Restoring More Than One File

You can choose to restore more than one file. For example, if you want to restore all files with a TXT extension to the \KEEP directory, the command to type is

RESTORE A: C:\KEEP*.TXT

The wild card *.TXT selects all files with the TXT extension from the KEEP directory. If you want to restore all files in a directory and all subdirectories below the directory, use the /S switch. The command **RESTORE A: C:\KEEP*.* /S** restores all files in directories subordinate to the \KEEP directory.

The following directory trees show the results of using selective BACKUP and RESTORE commands. Note that when you use the RESTORE command in the same way as the BACKUP command, RESTORE acts on the same files.

8

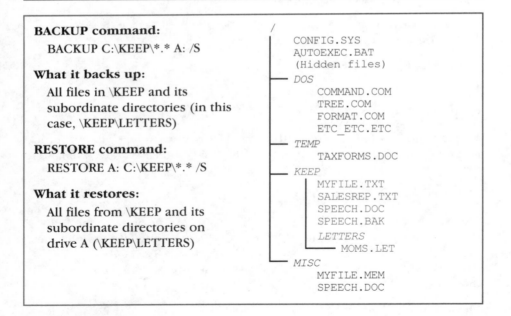

BACKUP Command:

    BACKUP C:*.* A: /S

What it backs up:

    All files on drive C

RESTORE command:

    RESTORE A: C:*.* /S

What it restores:

    All files from drive A, including subdirectories

```
/
    CONFIG.SYS
    AUTOEXEC.BAT
    (Hidden files)
─── DOS
        COMMAND.COM
        TREE.COM
        FORMAT.COM
        ETC_ETC.ETC
─── TEMP
        TAXFORMS.DOC
─── KEEP
        MYFILE.TXT
        SALESREP.TXT
        SPEECH.DOC
        SPEECH.BAK
        LETTERS
            ─── MOMS.LET
─── MISC
        MYFILE.MEM
        SPEECH.DOC
```

8

BACKUP command:

    BACKUP C:\KEEP*.* A: /S

What it backs up:

    All files in \KEEP and its subordinate directories (in this case, \KEEP\LETTERS)

RESTORE command:

    RESTORE A: C:\KEEP*.* /S

What it restores:

    All files from \KEEP and its subordinate directories on drive A (\KEEP\LETTERS)

```
/
    CONFIG.SYS
    AUTOEXEC.BAT
    (Hidden files)
─── DOS
        COMMAND.COM
        TREE.COM
        FORMAT.COM
        ETC_ETC.ETC
─── TEMP
        TAXFORMS.DOC
─── KEEP
        MYFILE.TXT
        SALESREP.TXT
        SPEECH.DOC
        SPEECH.BAK
        LETTERS
            ─── MOMS.LET
─── MISC
        MYFILE.MEM
        SPEECH.DOC
```

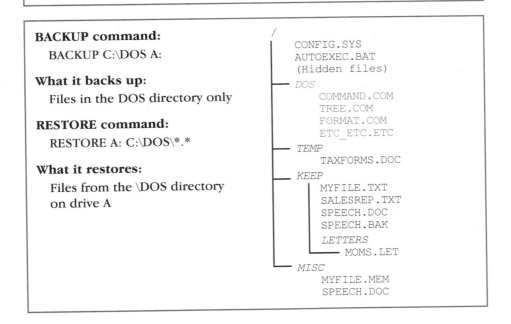

BACKUP command:

  BACKUP C:*.DOC A: /S

What it backs up:

  All files on drive C: with DOC
  extensions

RESTORE command:

  RESTORE A: C:*.DOC /S

What it restores:

  All files from drive A that have
  DOC extensions

```
/
    CONFIG.SYS
    AUTOEXEC.BAT
    (Hidden files)
  ┬ DOS
  │     COMMAND.COM
  │     TREE.COM
  │     FORMAT.COM
  │     ETC_ETC.ETC
  ┼ TEMP
  │     TAXFORMS.DOC
  ┼ KEEP
  │     MYFILE.TXT
  │     SALESREP.TXT
  │     SPEECH.DOC
  │     SPEECH.BAK
  │     LETTERS
  │      └── MOMS.LET
  └ MISC
        MYFILE.MEM
        SPEECH.DOC
```

BACKUP command:

  BACKUP C:\DOS A:

What it backs up:

  Files in the DOS directory only

RESTORE command:

  RESTORE A: C:\DOS*.*

What it restores:

  Files from the \DOS directory
  on drive A

```
/
    CONFIG.SYS
    AUTOEXEC.BAT
    (Hidden files)
  ┬ DOS
  │     COMMAND.COM
  │     TREE.COM
  │     FORMAT.COM
  │     ETC_ETC.ETC
  ┼ TEMP
  │     TAXFORMS.DOC
  ┼ KEEP
  │     MYFILE.TXT
  │     SALESREP.TXT
  │     SPEECH.DOC
  │     SPEECH.BAK
  │     LETTERS
  │      └── MOMS.LET
  └ MISC
        MYFILE.MEM
        SPEECH.DOC
```

8

Avoiding DOS Version Conflicts

Starting with version 3.3, DOS has a different method for producing the contents of a backup disk. DOS versions 3.3 and later can restore files that you backed up with previous versions of DOS. Versions earlier than 3.3, however, cannot restore backups made with versions 3.3 or 4.XX.

Although you cannot take backed up files from newer versions of DOS and restore them on computers running early versions of DOS, you can use COPY to move the files. Also, if you restore all files from a full backup to a computer running a different DOS version, the hidden system files and utility command programs from the backup files will overwrite the system files and utility command programs already on the hard drive. Finally, the RESTORE program from other MS-DOS vendors may simply not work with your version of DOS.

Lessons Learned

- Computers can be adversely affected by heat and humidity.
- In certain circumstances, both you and your PC can make mistakes.
- You can prevent many hardware and software failures.
- DOS's BACKUP utility allows you to make an exact backup of your hard disk drive.
- DOS's RESTORE utility allows you to restore several files or the entire contents of your hard disk drive.
- The newest releases of DOS (V3.3 or V4.XX) are capable of restoring files backed up by older releases. The reverse is not true, however.

DOS provides utilities that supply valuable information and services with just a few simple keystrokes. It's time now to review some of DOS's "nifty helpers."

Nifty Helpers

One of the more intimidating areas of DOS involves handling the dozens of files contained on a disk. When you first sat at a keyboard, you probably felt that manipulating this hodgepodge of programs was beyond the grasp of all but the most fanatical enthusiast.

Although DOS contains dozens of commands, some are more useful than others. Many long-time DOS users rarely utilize more than half of DOS's commands. This chapter looks at the more common DOS commands that you will need in your computing. Think of these commands as your DOS "survival" tools. Not only do these commands offer more control over your PC, but they also keep you informed of potential problems.

Topics in this chapter may appear a bit exotic—even unnecessary—but they are important to know about. If the FORMAT, COPY, DELETE, MKDIR, and RMDIR commands are DOS power tools, then the commands covered in this chapter are DOS screwdrivers, wrenches, and flashlights. After all, you don't need power tools to tighten screws or to change light bulbs.

You will find that with just a few DOS commands, you can do most of your work. This chapter also covers DOS devices and redirection. The section on redirection will teach you how to change both the standard source and standard destination of input and output.

Redirecting the input and output of DOS commands

Creating text files using the CONsole device

Using the CHKDSK command

Getting a DOS report on available memory

Key Terms Used in This Chapter

Redirection   Taking input from some place other than the keyboard or sending output to some place other than the screen.

Device   A hardware component or peripheral that DOS can use in some commands as though it were a file.

Console   The device DOS uses for keyboard input and screen output. DOS recognizes the console as CON.

ASCII file   A file whose contents are alphanumeric and control characters, which can be text or other information readable by humans.

Pipe   A method of taking the output of one command and making it the input for another command in DOS.

Filter   A method of selecting certain outputs from complete inputs.

DOS Devices and Redirection

In DOS, the term *redirection* means to change the source or destination normally used for input and output. The standard source of input is the keyboard. The standard output location is the screen display. When you use the keyboard to type a command, COMMAND.COM carries the text or messages and displays them on-screen. In DOS, the keyboard and display are the standard, or default, *devices* for messages, prompts, and input.

DOS views devices as extensions of the main unit of the computer.

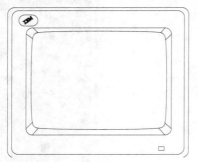

Display

Keyboard

9

Some devices send input and receive output, and some do both. Other devices are used for input only (the keyboard) or output only (the video display or printer).

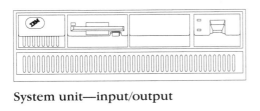

System unit—input/output

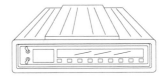

Modem—input/output

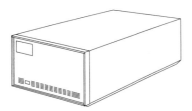

Disk drive—input/output

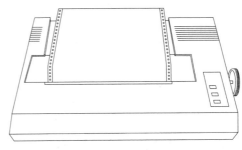

Printer—output

Disk drives are both input and output devices. Keyboards are input devices, but displays and printer adapters are output devices. Serial adapters can send output and receive input.

You can use device names (see table 9.1), as you do file names, in some commands. In fact, DOS treats devices as if they were files. Device names are three to four characters long and do not contain extensions. You cannot delete device names or format them, but you can use device names in commands to perform some useful actions.

9

Table 9.1
DOS Device Names

Name	Device
CON	The video display and keyboard.
AUX or COM1	The first asynchronous communications port. If a second asynchronous port is available, it is called COM2.
LPT1 or PRN	The first line or parallel printer. This device is used only for output.
LPT2	The second parallel printer.
LPT3	The third parallel printer.
NUL	A dummy device for redirecting output to "nowhere."

DOS controls devices through its system files and the ROM BIOS. Fortunately, understanding the details of how DOS handles devices is not essential to using them with DOS commands.

The COPY CON Device

A useful application for a DOS device is creating a file containing characters you input directly from the keyboard. To do so, you use the familiar COPY command. This time, however, you copy data from CON, the *CONsole* device.

CON is DOS's device name for the keyboard. In this case, suppose that you want to create a file named TEST.TXT. Follow these steps to send characters directly to the file:

1. At the DOS prompt type the following:

    COPY CON: TEST.TXT

    You have just told DOS: "Copy data from the console and send the output to the file TEST.TXT."

2. Press ⏎Enter)

    The cursor drops to the next line and no DOS prompt appears.

3. Begin typing characters as the input to the file.

    For example, type the following text: **This is a file copied quickly between a disk and a device.**

172

4. Press ⏎Enter

When you press ⏎Enter, DOS holds the line you typed in RAM.

5. Type several lines, if you want, pressing ⏎Enter after each line.

6. When you finish typing text, press F6 or Ctrl Z

DOS recognizes F6 or Ctrl-Z as the end-of-file character.

```
A>COPY CON TEST.TXT
This is a file copied quickly between a disk and a device.
^Z
        1 File(s) copied

A>
```

When you press F6 or Ctrl-Z, DOS saves the information you typed as a new file and displays the 1 File(s) copied message.

You can create simple files quickly with this method. However, as the length of a file increases, so does the desirability of using a text editor that has a nondocument mode. With COPY CON, you cannot go back to a previous line and correct it once you have pressed Enter. If you notice that an error was typed on a previous line, you have a couple of options:

- Hold down the Ctrl key and press the Break key. This ends the COPY CON operation. All the characters you typed will be lost.

- If you see an error after you saved the file, either delete the file and start over or use a line editor, such as Edlin, to correct the mistake.

Something else to remember is that you need to close your file, either with the F6 or with the Ctrl and Z keys. Until this is done, DOS assumes you are still typing characters into the file.

To be sure that the new file exists, do a directory listing with DIR and look for the file name TEST.TXT.

9

173

You have just entered a text file into your computer using a DOS command and a device name. With another DOS command, you can read the file's contents.

Displaying a Text File with TYPE

To display the contents of the new text file, use the DOS TYPE command. TYPE tells DOS to send the contents of a file to the display. At the DOS prompt, type

   TYPE TEST.TXT

```
A>TYPE TEST.TXT
This is a file copied quickly between a disk and a device.

A>
```

DOS takes input from the TEST.TXT file up to the end-of-file marker and displays it on your screen.

The TYPE command works on text files, or ASCII files. Don't bother trying the TYPE command to display files with the extensions COM and EXE. Both of these extensions are for program files and refer to binary files. The extensions MOS and OVL are also binary files. Using the TYPE command on a binary file shows nothing but gibberish.

Redirection Symbols

You must use special redirection symbols to tell DOS to use non-default devices in a command. Table 9.2 lists the symbols DOS recognizes for redirection.

174

Table 9.2
The Symbols for Redirection

Symbol	Description
<	Redirects a program's input
>	Redirects a program's output
> >	Redirects a program's output but adds the text to an established file.

The < symbol points away from the device or file and says, "Take input from here." The > symbol points toward the device or file and says, "Put output there." The > > symbol redirects a program's output, but adds the text to an established file. When you issue a redirection command, place the redirection symbol after the DOS command, but before the device name.

Redirecting to a Printer

Wouldn't it be practical to get the output of a DIR or TREE command on your printer? You can, by redirecting output to the device PRN (the printer). Make sure that you have the printer turned on and connected to your computer. Now type

DIR /W > PRN

When you press Enter, the output of the DIR command goes to the printer. The /W (wide display) switch lists the files in five columns. You can tuck such a printout into the sleeve of a floppy disk to identify the contents of a disk. If you entered text into the TEST.TXT file and your printer is ready, type the command

TYPE TEST.TXT > PRN

You now have a printed copy of the TEST.TXT file.

Never try to redirect binary files to the printer. Redirecting binary data can result in paper feed problems, beeps, meaningless graphics characters, and maybe a locked computer. If you get "hung," you can do a warm boot or turn the power switch off and then on again. If you must turn your computer off, it is good practice to wait about 15 seconds before turning it back on.

9

Pipes and Filters

The output of one command can be presented as the input of another
command. The pipe symbol (|) presents, or *pipes*, output from one
command to another. (By the way, don't confuse the pipe symbol with the
colon symbol.) The FIND, SORT, and MORE commands are *filters*. A filter is
a program that gets data from the standard input, changes the data, and then
writes the modified data to the display.

FIND, SORT, and MORE accept the output of a DOS command and do
further processing on that output. FIND outputs lines that match characters
given on the command line. SORT alphabetizes output. MORE displays a
prompt when each screen of the output is full.

One handy way of using the FIND filter is to get a directory listing that shows
only the directories. The following command is the one you use:

    DIR | FIND "<DIR>"

The FIND com-
mand filters the
output of a DIR
command. FIND
displays on-
screen only the
lines that contain
<DIR>. The |
symbol pipes the
output of DIR to
FIND.

```
A>DIR : FIND "DIR"
DOS          <DIR>      09-21-90    4:38p
TEMP         <DIR>      09-21-90    4:38p
KEEP         <DIR>      09-21-90    4:38p
MISC         <DIR>      09-21-90    4:38p

A>
```

The SORT command is a filter that alphabetizes its input. In the following
command, the output of the DIR command is piped to SORT:

    DIR | SORT

9

176

```
A>DIR : SORT

      14 File(s)     802304 bytes free
 Directory of  A:\
 Volume in drive A has no label
 Volume Serial Number is 4255-18C8
1136244C              0 09-21-90   5:54p
11362556              0 09-21-90   5:54p
CIM      CFG        490 08-08-90   1:51p
DOS           <DIR>     09-21-90   5:03p
FAM      HLP      15834 11-22-89  11:40a
FAVORITE DAT        305 08-08-90   4:51p
KEEP          <DIR>     09-21-90   5:03p
KEYBOARD LAY       1167 09-26-89   4:29p
MISC          <DIR>     09-21-90   5:04p
MOLES    DAT         28 11-22-89  10:32a
SAT      EXE     388157 11-21-89   1:24p
SET      COM         58 08-31-89   4:32p
TEMP          <DIR>     09-21-90   5:04p
UNTITLED TXT        227 08-06-90   3:47p

A>
```

When the directory listing, filtered by SORT, is displayed on the screen, it is in alphabetical order.

If a file is so long that the text scrolls off the screen, you can pause the display with Ctrl-S (or with the Pause key on Enhanced keyboards). The MORE filter provides another alternative solution to this problem. MORE displays information one screenful at a time.

To see how MORE works, create a second file named TEST2.TXT, using the COPY CON command. Make sure that you create more than 23 lines of text. Accuracy and content isn't important; the file only needs to be long. After you save TEST2.TXT with the F6 key or the Ctrl and Z keys, enter the following command:

TYPE TEST2.TXT | MORE

MORE displays 23 lines of text and pauses while displaying the message ---More---. When you press any key, MORE displays the next screen of text.

9

177

```
This is a file created by a device and
displayed by the TYPE
command. This is a file created by a
device and displayed by the TYPE
command. This is a file created by a
device and displayed by the TYPE
command. This is a file created by a
device and displayed by the TYPE
command. This is a file created by a
device and displayed by the TYPE
command. This is a file created by a
device and displayed by the TYPE
command. This is a file created by a
device and displayed by the TYPE
-- More --

command.

This is a file created by a device and
displayed by the TYPE
command. This is a file created by a
device and displayed by the TYPE
command. This is a file created by a

A>
```

The MORE filter solves the problem of text scrolling off the screen before you can read it.

Other Useful Commands

The commands presented so far should improve your control over your computer. This section offers additional commands that you will find useful.

CLS (Clear Screen)

The internal CLS command erases or clears the display and positions the cursor at the top left corner of the blank screen. Use CLS when the screen becomes too "busy" with the contents of previous commands' output. CLS has no parameters. You simply enter CLS at the DOS prompt, and the screen clears.

MEM (Memory Report)

The MEM command, new in DOS 4.XX, reports the amount of system memory available for programs to load and run.

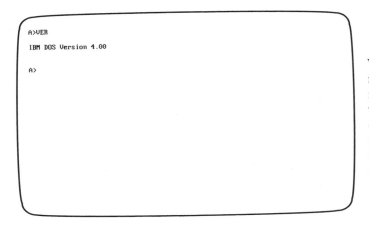

```
A>MEM

    655360 bytes total memory
    655360 bytes available
    425680 largest executable program size

A>
```

The MEM command tells the size of the largest program you can run.

In its simple form, you can issue MEM from the DOS prompt with no parameters. You can also redirect MEM's output to the PRN device.

VER (DOS Version)

You may find it useful to know the exact version of DOS your computer is running.

```
A>VER

IBM DOS Version 4.00

A>
```

VER reports a manufacturer's name and the version number of DOS. Your particular VER report may look slightly different.

9

VER is useful if you must work on another person's computer. You can issue this command before you start work to see which DOS version you will find in the computer. In this way, you know which commands or switches the computer accepts.

VER is also useful when you boot your system from a disk you did not prepare. The floppy may contain system files from a version of DOS you normally do not use. The VER command has no parameters and is issued at the DOS prompt.

VERIFY (File-Writing Verification)

VERIFY checks the accuracy of data written to disks. VERIFY has one parameter, which is ON or OFF. When you type **VERIFY ON** at the prompt, DOS rereads all data to insure that it was written correctly. VERIFY ON slows DOS operations; therefore you might want to use the command only with important data. Type **VERIFY OFF** to turn verification off again.

To display the status of VERIFY as being either on or off, type **VERIFY** and press Enter.

```
A>VERIFY
VERIFY is off

A>
```

VOL (Display Volume Name)

Recall that the /V switch used with the **FORMAT** command allows you to enter a disk volume name for a disk you want formatted.

9

```
A>VOL

  Volume in drive A is TESTDISK
  Volume Serial Number is 3A4D-1AD9

A>
```

When you type **VOL** at the DOS prompt, DOS displays the volume name of the current disk if you entered a name when you formatted the disk.

Viewing volume names is much easier than wading through directory listings when you sort through floppy disks.

CHKDSK (Check Disk)

CHKDSK is an external command that checks disk space and provides a detailed report of disk and memory status. CHKDSK also can repair certain errors on the disk.

The syntax for CHKDSK is

> **CHKDSK** *d:path\filename.ext* **/F/V**

The *d:* is the drive that contains the disk you want to check. The *path* is the directory and *filename.ext* is the file name. The /F switch tells DOS to fix problems on the disk if it finds errors. The /V switch is the verbose switch. The /V switch causes DOS to display detailed information about any errors detected.

Because CHKDSK is an external command, you must specify its directory location with the PATH command or give the path on the command line.

9

```
C:\>CHKDSK

Volume BILLS ACER  created 07-24-1990 8:10p
Volume Serial Number is 3E40-1BCF

 97728512 bytes total disk space
   120832 bytes in 7 hidden files
   143360 bytes in 55 directories
 53735424 bytes in 2120 user files
 43728896 bytes available on disk

     2048 bytes in each allocation unit
    47719 total allocation units on disk
    21352 available allocation units on disk

   655360 total bytes memory
   389344 bytes free

C:\>
```

CHKDSK repeats
disk and file in-
formation.

You can use wild cards in the file specifier with CHKDSK. If you omit the
names of the disk and directory, the command uses the DOS defaults.

You can redirect the output of CHKDSK to the printer if you do not use the
/F switch. Redirecting CHKDSK's output to the printer is a practical way to
preserve the information generated by the command. To do this, type the
following command:

   CHKDSK > PRN

CHKDSK /F

Proper use of the /F switch is a common "fix" to convert lost clusters on disks
into files. When used, the /F switch can occasionally recover important data
you may have lost.

```
C:\>CHKDSK /F

Volume BILLS ACER  created 07-24-1990 8:10p
Volume Serial Number is 3E40-1BCF

   138 lost allocation units found in 2 chains.
Convert lost chains to files (Y/N)?Y

 97728512 bytes total disk space
   120832 bytes in 7 hidden files
   143360 bytes in 55 directories
 53618688 bytes in 2116 user files
   282624 bytes in 2 recovered files
 43563008 bytes available on disk

     2048 bytes in each allocation unit
    47719 total allocation units on disk
    21271 available allocation units on disk

   655360 total bytes memory
   389888 bytes free

C:\>
```

The /F switch
causes DOS to
ask you before it
fixes problems
the command
has detected.

182

CHKDSK assigns these files names as shown on-screen. Files no longer useful may be safely deleted.

```
C:\>DIR *.CHK

 Volume in drive C is BILLS ACER
 Volume Serial Number is 3E40-1BCF
 Directory of  C:\

FILE0000 CHK      4096 09-12-90  12:06p
FILE0001 CHK    278528 09-12-90  12:06p
        2 File(s)   43563008 bytes free

C:\>
```

CHKDSK converts clusters into files with the name FILEnnnn, where FILEnnnn stands for FILE0000, FILE0001, FILE0002, and so on.

Avoid using /F until you know the implications of the fix action. *MS-DOS V5 User's Guide* explains the /F switch actions in detail. You should consult this book if CHKDSK finds problems.

CHKDSK before a Backup

One useful feature of CHKDSK is its ability to report the number of bytes used in directories, user files, and hidden files. You can use CHKDSK before you issue the BACKUP command to determine the number of bytes to be backed up. You can then determine the number of floppy disks you need for the backup.

Space on floppy disks is usually measured in kilobytes or megabytes. Divide the total number of bytes to be backed up by 1000 for kilobytes, or by 1,000,000 for megabytes. Divide the number of kilobytes or megabytes by the capacity of your backup floppies to find out how many disks you will need to complete the backup.

For example, suppose that you want to back up a hard disk but don't know how many floppies to prepare. You can issue the command **CHKDSK C:** and DOS will check the directory on your logged disk and issue a report.

9

183

The report gives you the disk's total capacity in bytes, the number of hidden files and their byte total, the number of directories and their byte total, and the number of user files and their byte total. The report also gives the total memory bytes in RAM and the number of RAM bytes free for use.

If you add the number of bytes in hidden files, directories, and user files, you have the number of bytes to be backed up. Normally the hidden files and directory files do not add up to more than 100K. You will be safe using the user files total to calculate the number of floppies you need for a backup.

Remember, the number of disks required is based on their capacity to hold a specific amount of data. A 1.2M floppy holds four times the data of a 360K disk. Verify that the disks used have the capacity you expect. Double-check disk labels for the correct density, and watch for bad sectors when formatting floppy disks.

CHKDSK and Fragmentation

One of the messages given by CHKDSK concerns noncontiguous blocks in files. This condition is *fragmentation*, which you may recall from Chapter 7. Fragmentation means that as you delete and add disk files, gaps occur. A new file cannot always be stored in a single space on the disk.

9

CHKDSK reports whether a file is fragmented—that is, not stored in contiguous blocks. In this example, SAMPLES.TXT is the file on which CHKDSK reports.

```
C:\>CHKDSK SAMPLES.TXT

Volume BILLS ACER  created 07-24-1990 8:10p
Volume Serial Number is 3E40-1BCF

  97728512 bytes total disk space
    120832 bytes in 7 hidden files
    143360 bytes in 55 directories
  53735424 bytes in 2120 user files
  43728896 bytes available on disk

      2048 bytes in each allocation unit
     47719 total allocation units on disk
     21352 available allocation units on disk

    655360 total bytes memory
    389344 bytes free

C:\SAMPLES.TXT Contains 7 non-contiguous blocks

C:\>
```

184

Fragmentation is not serious. It happens to all active disks. At worst, fragmentation slows down disk operations slightly. See Chapter 7 for information on dealing with fragmented disks.

Lessons Learned

■ You are likely to use only half of DOS's commands. Some people use even fewer.

■ A device is computer hardware other than the main unit, such as the keyboard, video display, or printer.

■ COPY CON allows you to create a file directly from your keyboard, without using a text editor.

■ The PRN device allows you to direct printing from your keyboard to the printer without using a word processing program or text editor.

■ Such DOS commands as MEM, VER, CHKDSK, and VOL are quick commands for controlling and monitoring your hardware and software.

Now, let's add some personality to your PC with batch, CONFIG.SYS, and AUTOEXEC.BAT files.

9

9

Adding Personality to Your PC

Of all the criticisms hurled at DOS, perhaps the most damaging complaint is that DOS feels inherently cold. The basic screen contains nothing more than a command prompt. You see neither hint nor whisper of what you should do next.

This chapter involves what might be called electronic "personality development," because you really can act as psychiatrist and plastic surgeon for your PC. You can make working with your computer lively or dull, somber or splashy. Your most useful tool is the batch file.

Key Terms Used in This Chapter

Batch file
A text file that contains DOS commands, which DOS executes as though the commands were entered at the DOS prompt. Batch files always have a BAT extension.

Meta-string
A series of characters that takes on a different meaning to DOS than the literal meaning. DOS displays substitute text when it finds meta-strings in the PROMPT command.

AUTOEXEC.BAT file
An optional but helpful batch file that is located in the root directory of a boot disk. AUTOEXEC.BAT is an ideal place to include commands that initialize and personalize the control of a PC.

CONFIG.SYS file
A file whose contents are used by DOS to tailor hardware devices and to assign the computer's resources.

Buffer
An area of RAM allocated by DOS as a temporary storage area for data that is moving between the disks and an executing program.

Directive
A command-like DOS element that establishes the status or value of a system setting that can be modified. Unlike commands, directives don't execute an action. Rather, they set values.

10

This chapter is not designed to make you a batch file expert, although you might be surprised to find how much you can learn in a few pages. If you've read this far, you are now a reasonably skilled DOS user. Here, you will learn how to create and modify batch, AUTOEXEC.BAT, and CONFIG.SYS files. Also included here are some useful sample batch files.

Defining the Batch File

A *batch file* is a text file that contains DOS commands. DOS executes these commands one line at a time, treating them as though you had issued each command individually.

Batch files always have the extension BAT in their full file names. When you type a batch file's name at the DOS prompt, COMMAND.COM looks in the current directory for a filename with the BAT extension. COMMAND.COM then reads the file and executes the DOS commands the file contains. The whole process is automatic. You enter the batch file name, and DOS does the work.

Computer programmers frequently demean the batch file. They prefer spending weeks writing complex programs ending in EXE or COM, rather than batch files. Often, they prefer complexity to common sense.

Nobody says that batch files can accomplish everything, because they can't. However, programmers too often view simplicity as an affront to their skill. They forget that a batch file can easily create a pleasant, interactive link between people and their PCs.

The batch file varies from being the most ignored to being the most abused of all programs. Many books are devoted to the batch file's capabilities, some to a point where readers walk away scratching their heads in confusion. In truth, you should consider the batch file to be the nonprogrammer's programming language. It is a limited yet powerful language: each word can have the power of several lines of DOS commands with the power of programming code.

You can review the contents of a batch file by simply typing the TYPE command. In seconds, you can alter a file that changes your PC's personality profile.

10

Batch files are also useful for issuing multiple commands that are complex, potentially destructive, or easy to mistype at the command line. A good example would be some form of the BACKUP command with several switches.

BACKUP is a simple command, but it can be confusing, since you probably don't use it often. You may find it more convenient to put properly formed backup commands in batch files that you can execute with one simple batch name. This chapter contains a batch file for a full system backup that you can use as presented or change to fit your own situation.

Because batch files can display text that you enter, you can compose screens that allow you to execute commands, along with syntax examples, reminders, and explanatory notes about the commands. Also, you can simply display a message of the day.

In their advanced form, batch files resemble programs. In this chapter you'll learn about useful forms of batch files. If advanced techniques in batch processing interests you, be sure to read about batch files in *MS-DOS User's Guide*, Special Edition.

Creating a Batch File

Batch files contain ASCII text characters. You can create a text file with many word processing programs in nondocument mode.

Nondocument mode is a setting that omits special formatting and control characters which word processing programs use for internal purposes. Composing batch files in nondocument mode eliminates errors in syntax that the special characters might cause.

You also may use the DOS line editor, EDLIN, to create a batch file. The easiest way to create a batch file, however, is to use the COPY CON device. Just remember that COPY CON does not allow you to correct a text line after you strike the Enter key.

Caution: Never choose a name for your batch file that is the same as that of a DOS external command. If you do, DOS will run the batch file instead of the command.

10

Creating a Batch File with COPY CON

Using COPY CON, you can create a batch file that clears the screen and presents a wide directory. This batch file automates the CLS screen clear command and the DIR command with the /W (wide display) switch.

1. If you have a hard disk, use the CD command to change to the directory that contains your DOS external commands.

2. Type **COPY CON WDIR.BAT** and press ⏎Enter

   The cursor drops to the next line, and DOS waits for your keyboard input.

   Make sure that you type each line correctly. Use the Backspace key to correct mistakes and then press ⏎Enter. If you do make a mistake and press ⏎Enter, press Ctrl C and resume the process from this step.

3. Type **CLS** and press ⏎Enter

4. Type **DIR /W** and press ⏎Enter

5. Type Ctrl Z (hold down the Ctrl key and type Z) or press the F6 function key.

6. Press ⏎Enter

   DOS displays the message 1 File(s) copied.

```
A>CD \DOS

A>COPY CON WDIR.BAT
CLS
DIR /W
^Z
        1 File(s) copied

A>
```

10

The Wide Direc-
tory batch file

To see that the directory contains the new batch file, type **DIR WDIR.BAT** and press Enter. To try out the batch file, type **WDIR** and press Enter. The screen clears, and the directory displays in its wide form. You have just created a new DOS batch file, using COPY CON.

Creating a Batch File with a Word Processing Program

Creating a batch file using a word processing program is even easier than using COPY CON.

1. Start your word processing program.
2. Create a nondocument file, making sure the file name has the BAT extension.
3. Type **CLS** and press ↵Enter
4. Type **DIR /W**
5. Save your nondocument.

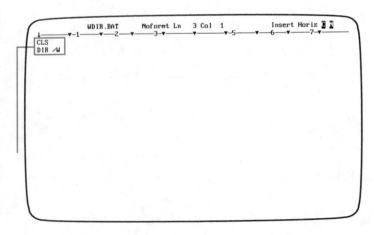

Using a word processor to create a batch file.

To try out the batch file, type **WDIR** at the system prompt and press Enter. The screen clears, and the directory displays in its wide form. You have just created a new DOS batch file using your word processor.

Rules for Batch Files

When you create batch files, you must follow certain rules. The following list is a summary of those rules.

- Batch files must be ASCII text files. If you use a word processor, make sure that it is in programming, or nondocument, mode. Many commercial DOS shells come with this type of line editor. You can start it with the tap of a key.
- The name of the batch file can be from one to eight characters long. The name must conform to the rules for naming files. It is best to use alphabetical characters in batch file names.
- The file name must end with the extender dot (.), followed by the BAT extension.
- The batch file name should not be the same as a program file name (a file with an EXE or COM extension).
- The batch file name should not be the same as an internal DOS command (such as COPY or DATE).
- The batch file can contain any DOS commands that you enter at the DOS prompt.
- You can include program names in the batch file that you usually type at the DOS prompt.
- Use only one command or program name per line in the batch file.

Rules for Running Batch Files

You start batch files by typing the batch file name (excluding the extension) at the DOS prompt. The following list summarizes the rules DOS follows when it loads and executes batch files.

- If you do not specify the disk drive name before the batch file name, DOS uses the current drive.
- If you do not give a path, DOS searches through the current directory for the batch file.
- If the batch file isn't in the current directory and you didn't precede the batch file name with a path, DOS searches the directories specified by the last PATH command you issued.

10

- If DOS finds a syntax error in a batch file command line, DOS displays an error message, skips the errant command, and then executes the remaining commands found in the batch file.
- You can stop a batch command with Ctrl-C or Ctrl-Break. DOS prompts you to confirm that you want to terminate the batch file. If you answer no, DOS skips the current command (the one being carried out) and resumes execution with the next command in the batch file.

If you try to run a batch file and DOS displays an error message, you probably made a mistake when you typed the name. You can view any batch file by using the TYPE *filename* command.

Understanding the AUTOEXEC.BAT File

One batch file has special significance to DOS. The full name of this batch file is *AUTOEXEC.BAT*. DOS automatically searches for this file in the root directory when you boot your computer. If an AUTOEXEC.BAT file is present, DOS executes the commands in the file.

Because the AUTOEXEC.BAT file is optional, not every PC has this file. However, most users or system managers add an AUTOEXEC.BAT file of their own design on their boot disk. Using a custom AUTOEXEC.BAT file allows them to benefit from commands that launch operating parameters automatically.

You could omit AUTOEXEC.BAT, manually enter the commands that you might include in an AUTOEXEC.BAT file, and accomplish the same result as an AUTOEXEC.BAT file. DOS, however, executes the file if it is there, so why not take advantage? As a rule, AUTOEXEC.BAT files are not distributed with the DOS package because different users need varied commands.

The installation process for DOS V4.0 creates a file called AUTOEXEC.400, which includes commands that you might want. By changing the name of the AUTOEXEC.400 file to AUTOEXEC.BAT, you enable DOS to execute the commands in the file after booting.

Some software comes with installation programs that create or modify AUTOEXEC.BAT as an installation step of the package's main program.

10

If you have doubts about what commands to include in your AUTOEXEC.BAT file, the following sections should give you some ideas. You can include any commands you want in the AUTOEXEC.BAT file. Decide what you want the AUTOEXEC.BAT file to do, and follow certain rules. The following list is a summary of these rules.

- The full file name must be AUTOEXEC.BAT and the file must reside in the root directory of the boot disk.
- The contents of the AUTOEXEC.BAT file must conform to the rules for creating any batch file.
- When DOS executes AUTOEXEC.BAT after a boot, you are not prompted for the date and time automatically. You must include the DATE and TIME commands in your AUTOEXEC.BAT file if you want to keep this step when booting.

Using AUTOEXEC.BAT is an excellent way for you to set up changeable system defaults. That is, AUTOEXEC.BAT is the place to put commands you would want to enter every time you start your system. For example, you can use AUTOEXEC.BAT to tell your computer to change to the directory that holds your most commonly used program and then to start it. Used this way, AUTOEXEC.BAT runs your program as soon as you boot your computer.

```
C:\>TYPE AUTOEXEC.BAT
DATE
TIME
PATH=C:\DOS;C:\KEEP;C:\;
PROMPT $P$G
DIR
CD \DOS
ECHO Good Day, Mate

C:\>
```

Here is an example of an AUTOEXEC.BAT file—a batch file whose commands DOS executes each time you boot the computer.

10

Table 10.1 lists the commands most frequently included in simple AUTOEXEC.BAT files. The table also explains each line of the batch file shown in the preceding figure.

195

Table 10.1
AUTOEXEC.BAT File Commands

Command	*Function in the AUTOEXEC.BAT File*
DATE	Uses the computer's clock to set up the correct date so that DOS can accurately "date stamp" new and modified files.
TIME	Uses the computer's clock to establish the correct time so that DOS can accurately "time stamp" new and modified files. The DATE and TIME commands also provide the actual date and time to programs that use the computer's internal clock.
PATH	Tells DOS to search the named subdirectories for files that have EXE, COM, or BAT extensions. Ends the need for the operator to enter the path through the keyboard after each boot. The example **PATH=C:\DOS;C:\KEEP;C:\;** tells DOS to search the subdirectories C:\DOS, C:\KEEP, and C:\.
PROMPT	Customizes the system prompt. The DOS prompt configuration can include information that makes navigating in directories easier. If you use the PROMPT command in the AUTOEXEC.BAT file, you won't need to enter the optional parameters each time you boot. In the example, **PROMPT PG** customized the prompt to show the current drive and path, and the greater than (>) symbol.
DIR	Shows a listing of the root directory as soon as the computer boots.
CD	When used with a directory path, takes you immediately to a specified directory. For example, **CD \DOS** makes \DOS the current directory.
ECHO	Allows you to include a message as part of your start-up when used in the AUTOEXEC.BAT file. On a floppy disk system, this message can remind you to insert a program disk in drive A. In the example, the message "Good Day, Mate" is displayed on-screen as part of the start-up procedure.

10

The PATH Command

You know how to issue the PATH command to tell DOS where to search for COM, EXE, and BAT files. In this section, you will learn how to put the PATH command that contains the search paths into the AUTOEXEC.BAT file. With this information, DOS knows the search path as soon as you boot the computer.

For example, suppose that you create a directory on your hard disk called \DOS. To tell DOS to search the \DOS directory, type

PATH C:\DOS

If you want DOS to search in the root directory first, the \DOS directory next, and another directory—such as \TEMP—last, type

PATH C:\;C:\DOS;C:\TEMP

Notice how semicolons separate the three directory names. The path you include in the AUTOEXEC.BAT file becomes DOS's default search path. Of course, you can change this default path. Simply issue the PATH command with a new path or set of paths at the DOS prompt.

The PROMPT Command

You know what your DOS prompt looks like, but did you know that you can change it? With the PROMPT command, you can change the DOS prompt to a wide variety of looks. The symbolic syntax for the PROMPT command is

PROMPT *text*

The *text* is any combination of words or special characters. The term used to describe the special characters is *meta-string*.

Understanding Meta-strings

A meta-string consists of two characters, the first is the dollar sign ($) and the second, a keyboard character. DOS interprets meta-strings to mean something other than the literal character definition. For instance, the meta-string $T in the PROMPT command tells DOS, "Display the current time, in

10

197

the HH:MM:SS.XX" format, in the DOS prompt. $T displays the current system time as part or all of the command prompt.

DOS recognizes the symbols >, <, and the vertical bar (|) as special characters. They all have meta-string equivalents so you can use them in PROMPT text. You must substitute an appropriate meta-string to cause these special characters to appear in the prompt. Otherwise, DOS tries to act on the characters in its usual way. Table 10.2 summarizes meta-string characters and their meanings to the PROMPT command.

Table 10.2
Meta-string Characters

Character	What it produces
$	$, the actual dollar sign
_ (underscore)	moves the cursor to the next line
B	the vertical bar	
D	the current date
G	the > character
L	the < character
N	the current disk drive name
P	the current drive and path
Q	the = character
T	the system time
V	the DOS version
Any other	the character is ignored

10

Customizing Your Prompt

You can use the meta-string characters with the PROMPT command to produce your own DOS prompt. PROMPT allows words or phrases in addition to meta-strings. You can experiment with different combinations of meta-strings and phrases.

When you find a combination that you favor, type the PROMPT command and the meta-string and phrase. Then, each time you boot your computer your custom prompt will appear. Issuing the PROMPT command alone with no parameters restores the prompt to its default, the drive name and the greater-than sign (C>).

If you want your prompt to tell you the current DOS path, type the command

PROMPT THE CURRENT PATH IS $P

If your current location is drive C in the DOS directory, this PROMPT command produces the following prompt

```
THE CURRENT PATH IS C:\DOS
```

By adding the > sign (using the meta-string $G), the command would be

PROMPT THE CURRENT PATH IS PG

Now your DOS prompt would appear as

```
THE CURRENT PATH IS C:\DOS>
```

Making an AUTOEXEC.BAT File

The AUTOEXEC.BAT file is a privileged batch file because DOS executes its batch of commands each time you boot your computer. In every other sense, however, AUTOEXEC.BAT is like any other batch file.

Most computers already have an AUTOEXEC.BAT file in the root directory of the hard disk or on the bootable floppy disk.

Viewing the AUTOEXEC.BAT File

You can easily see whether AUTOEXEC.BAT exists in your root directory or on your logged floppy disk. If your hard disk is the logged drive, change to the root directory by typing

CD

You can look at the directory listing of all the files with .BAT extensions by typing

DIR *.BAT

10

199

You can view the contents of AUTOEXEC.BAT on-screen by typing

TYPE AUTOEXEC.BAT

You also can get a printed copy of the AUTOEXEC.BAT file by redirecting output to the printer with the command

TYPE AUTOEXEC.BAT >PRN

If you choose not to print a copy of your AUTOEXEC.BAT file, make sure that you write down the contents before you make any changes. Be sure that you copy the syntax correctly. This copy will serve as your worksheet.

You can use your copy of AUTOEXEC.BAT to find out if a PROMPT or PATH command is contained in the batch file. If you want to add or alter PROMPT or PATH commands, jot the additions or changes on your worksheet. Use your paper copy of the AUTOEXEC.BAT file to check for proper syntax in the lines you change or add before you commit the changes to disk.

Backing Up the Existing File

Always make a backup copy of your existing AUTOEXEC.BAT file before you make any changes in the file. Save the current version by renaming it with a different extension.

Use the following procedure to file away your AUTOEXEC.BAT for future use:

1. Type **CD** and press (┘Enter) to change to the root directory.
2. Type **DIR *.BAT** and press (┘Enter) to check for the presence of an AUTOEXEC.BAT file.
3. Type **TYPE AUTOEXEC.BAT** and press (┘Enter) to display on-screen the contents of the existing AUTOEXEC.BAT file.
4. Type **RENAME AUTOEXEC.BAT AUTOEXEC.OLD**. Press (┘Enter) to save a copy of the original AUTOEXEC.BAT file under the new name AUTOEXEC.OLD.

The RENAME command transfers the name AUTOEXEC.BAT to the AUTOEXEC.OLD file. The name AUTOEXEC.BAT is now available for use with a new file.

10

If the new AUTOEXEC.BAT file does not work, or does not do what you want, you can always erase the new file. Then, using the RENAME command, you can rename the AUTOEXEC.OLD file AUTOEXEC.BAT and be back where you started:

ERASE AUTOEXEC.BAT

RENAME AUTOEXEC.OLD AUTOEXEC.BAT

Entering a New File

Now you are ready to use COPY CON to enter your new or revised AUTOEXEC.BAT file. Follow these steps:

1. Type the command **COPY CON AUTOEXEC.BAT**

2. Type the commands from your worksheet, one command per line. After you type each line, correct any mistakes, and then press ⏎Enter

   To create the batch file shown in the following figure, type the following lines, pressing ⏎Enter after each line:

   DATE
   TIME
   PATH=C:\DOS;C:\KEEP;C:
   CD \DOS

3. When you finish, press F6 or Ctrl Z to write the new file to disk.

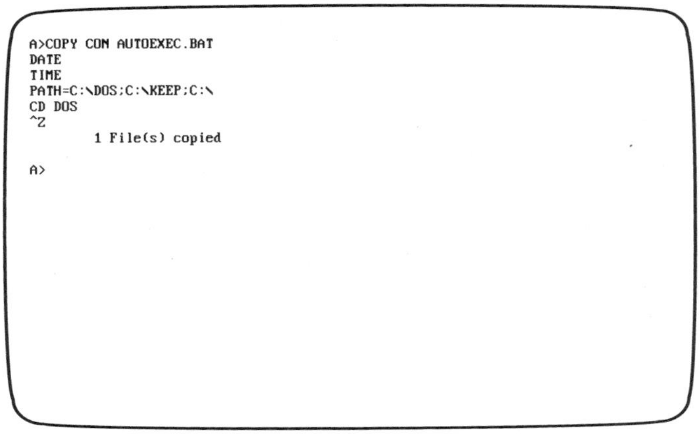

```
A>COPY CON AUTOEXEC.BAT
DATE
TIME
PATH=C:\DOS;C:\KEEP;C:\
CD DOS
^Z
        1 File(s) copied

A>
```

10

Using COPY CON, you can create a new AUTOEXEC.BAT file.

When you reboot (by pressing Ctrl-Alt-Del), DOS executes the commands in the new AUTOEXEC.BAT file. You can also run the AUTOEXEC.BAT file by typing **AUTOEXEC** at the system prompt.

Keeping Several Versions of AUTOEXEC

Technically speaking, there is only one AUTOEXEC.BAT file. You can benefit from having several "versions" on hand, by giving different extensions to files named AUTOEXEC. You can then activate an alternative version by using the RENAME and COPY commands.

You can use in the extensions any character that DOS normally allows in file names. The extensions BAK, OLD, NEW, TMP, and 001 are just a few examples. By giving an AUTOEXEC file a unique name, such as AUTOEXEC.TMP, you can activate any other AUTOEXEC file by renaming it AUTOEXEC.BAT.

This method is handy if you want to include commands for special activities, such as automatically starting a monthly spreadsheet. When the monthly work is done, and you no longer need the spreadsheet when you boot, you can reactivate your normal AUTOEXEC file by changing its temporary name back to AUTOEXEC.BAT.

Understanding the CONFIG.SYS File

AUTOEXEC.BAT is not the only file that DOS looks for when you boot your computer. DOS also looks for CONFIG.SYS. *CONFIG.SYS* is DOS's additional configuration file. Not only does DOS provide built-in services for disks and other hardware, it also extends its services for add-on hardware. The additional instructions that DOS needs to incorporate outside services, such as some devices, are included in the CONFIG.SYS file.

CONFIG.SYS is also the location for naming the values of DOS configuration items that can be "tuned." Files and buffers, discussed in the next section, are two "tunable" DOS items. CONFIG.SYS is a text file like AUTOEXEC.BAT; you can display it on-screen, or print it. You can also change the contents of CONFIG.SYS with the COPY CON command or with a text editor.

10

Although CONFIG.SYS is not a batch file, it is very similar to one. DOS does not execute CONFIG.SYS as it does AUTOEXEC.BAT. Instead, DOS reads the values in the file and configures your computer to agree with those values. Many software packages modify or add a CONFIG.SYS file to the root directory. The range of possible values in the file is wide, but there are some common values that you can include.

Specifying Files and Buffers

When DOS moves data to and from disks, it does so in the most efficient manner possible. For each file that DOS acts upon, there is an area of system RAM that helps DOS track the operating details of that file. The number of built-in RAM areas for this tracking operation is controlled by the FILES directive in CONFIG.SYS. (A *directive* establishes in the CONFIG.SYS file the value of a system setting that can be modified.) If a program tries to open more files than the FILES directive setting allows, DOS will tell you too many files are open.

Do not be tempted to set your FILES directive to a large number just so you will always have room for more open files. The system RAM for programs is reduced by each extra file included in FILES. As a rule of thumb, a good compromise is 20 open files. The line you type in CONFIG.SYS to set the number of open files to 20 is

FILES=20

Similar to the FILES directive is the BUFFERS directive. *Buffers* are holding areas in RAM that store information coming from or going to disk files. To make the disk operation more efficient, DOS stores disk information in file buffers in RAM. It then uses RAM, instead of the disk drives, for input and output whenever possible.

10

If the file information needed is not already in the buffer, new information is read into the buffer from the disk file. The information that DOS reads includes the needed information and as much additional file information as the buffer will hold. With this buffer of needed information, there is a good chance that DOS can avoid constant disk access. The principle is similar to the way a mechanic might use a small tool pouch. Holding frequently used tools in a small pouch relieves him of having to make repeated trips across the garage to get tools from his main tool chest.

Like the FILES directive, however, setting the BUFFERS directive too high takes needed RAM away from programs and dedicates it to the buffers. As a rule, 20 buffers should work effectively for you. On the other hand, some of the better commercial backup programs request more.

To include the FILES and BUFFERS directives in the CONFIG.SYS file during the COPY CON command, type **FILES=20** and press Enter. Then type **BUFFERS=20** on the next line. Remember, some programs make their own changes to FILES and BUFFERS in the CONFIG.SYS file. Most applications software tells you what the values of FILES and BUFFERS should be. Check your program manual for details.

You can use FILES and BUFFERS settings above 20 with DOS 3.3 and 4.0. As a rule, however, do not use a setting of more than 20 unless the program documentation instructs you to.

Designating Device Drivers

You'll recall that DOS works with peripherals, such as disk drives, printers, and displays. These peripherals are also called devices. DOS has built-in instructions, called *drivers*, to handle these devices.

Some devices, such as a mouse, are foreign to DOS. DOS lacks the built-in ability to handle them. To issue directions to devices that DOS doesn't recognize, use the DEVICE directive. The syntax for this directive is:

DEVICE=*device driver file name*

For example, the device driver for a mouse can be in a file called MOUSE.SYS. So that DOS understands how to use the mouse, you would enter a command like this:

DEVICE=MOUSE.SYS

The DEVICE directive tells DOS to find and load the driver program for the new device. Then, DOS can control the device.

Most peripherals come with a disk that contains a device-driver file. This file contains the necessary instructions to control, or drive, the device. The device-driver disk usually contains a provision to modify your CONFIG.SYS file to include the proper DEVICE directive.

10

The device driver is often copied from the device's installation disk to a new subdirectory that the installation program creates. The DEVICE directive will then include the full path to the driver so DOS can locate it.

If you copy a device driver file to its own subdirectory, use the full path to the driver file as you type the DEVICE directive into the CONFIG.SYS file. For example, suppose that you install a Microsoft Mouse device driver called MOUSE.SYS in a directory named \DOS\DRIVERS. You would add the following line in your CONFIG.SYS file:

> **DEVICE=\DOS\DRIVERS\MOUSE.SYS**

This directive activates your mouse driver (and your mouse) when you boot. Always check your program and hardware manuals before experimenting with your system. Many programs provide prepared device directives for you.

Making a CONFIG.SYS File

You should back up your disk before you add to or change a CONFIG.SYS file. Make sure that the CONFIG.SYS file is in your root directory, or on your boot floppy. If your directory contains CONFIG.SYS, use the TYPE command to see the contents of the file on the screen. If you have a printer, you can redirect the TYPE command's output to the printer. Use a printout or a written copy of the CONFIG.SYS file as a worksheet to write the directives you want to change or include.

If you need to change your CONFIG.SYS file, rename it CONFIG.OLD. Now you can use the command COPY CON CONFIG.SYS to make a new version. Type your directives from your worksheet and pay close attention to syntax. When you finish, press F6 or Ctrl-Z. After you reboot your computer, the new configuration will take effect. If you get DOS error messages, display your new CONFIG.SYS file with the TYPE command and check for mistakes. If you find errors, erase the file and use COPY CON to type the lines again. A sample CONFIG.SYS file might contain these lines:

> **FILES=20**
> **BUFFERS=20**
> **DEVICE=\DOS\DRIVERS\MOUSE.SYS**
> **DEVICE=\DOS\DRIVERS\ANSI.SYS**

10

Each of these lines is explained in the text that follows:

FILES=20

> Establishes 20 built-in RAM areas for DOS to track the operating
> system details of open files. If a program you use tries to open
> more than 20 files, DOS will tell you too many files are open.

BUFFERS=20

> Sets up 20 holding areas in RAM that store information coming
> from or going to disk files. DOS then uses RAM, instead of the disk
> drives, for input and output whenever possible.

DEVICE=\DOS\DRIVERS\MOUSE.SYS

> Tells DOS how to handle a peripheral device—in this case, a mouse.

DEVICE=\DOS\DRIVERS\ANSI.SYS

> Identifies American National Standards Institute screen-control
> character sequences.

Your CONFIG.SYS file might contain other device drivers and DOS settings.
Because the subdirectories on each computer may vary, the exact contents of
CONFIG.SYS device directives will vary. If you want to explore configurations
and device concepts in more detail, consult *MS-DOS V5 User's Guide*. If you
are unsure about the device drivers for new peripherals you buy, ask your
dealer how to incorporate the new device.

Creating Sample Batch Files

If you are a beginner, you may benefit from entering sample batch files.
Practicing with the following examples will make it easier to understand how
to construct your own DOS batch files.

Simplified Backup Using a Batch File

You know how important it is to back up your files. Perhaps a batch file that
issues the command to back up your entire hard disk would be useful. You
can execute this batch file once a month, or every other week, to keep a
snapshot of your hard disk.

This batch file uses the ECHO command to send text to your display. ECHO
OFF stops the echoing of the DOS commands in the file. Using ECHO OFF
keeps the screen uncluttered by the commands as the file executes. The
screen does, however, display text that is the result of an ECHO command.

10

The PAUSE command is used to suspend the execution of the batch file until you press a key. Using the COPY CON method, create the following file in your DOS disk or directory:

```
COPY CON BIGBACK.BAT
ECHO OFF
CLS
ECHO ************************************************************
ECHO *                                                          *
ECHO * YOU ARE ABOUT TO INITIATE A FULL BACKUP OF YOUR HARD DISK *
ECHO *                                                          *
ECHO * You will be asked to insert floppy disks into drive A.   *
ECHO *                                                          *
ECHO * Please have your floppies ready before proceeding.       *
ECHO *                                                          *
ECHO * IF YOU DON'T WANT TO PROCEED, ENTER Ctrl-C TO STOP       *
ECHO * AND ANSWER 'Y' TO THE TERMINATION PROMPT THAT WILL       *
ECHO * FOLLOW CTRL C.                                           *
ECHO *                                                          *
ECHO ************************************************************
ECHO ^G (entered as Ctrl+G on keyboard to produce a beep)
PAUSE
CLS
ECHO ** FULL HARD DISK BACKUP IN PROGRESS. . . Ctrl-C to Stop    **
ECHO ON
\DOS\BACKUP C:\*.* A:/S
ECHO OFF
CLS
ECHO **           THE FULL BACKUP OPERATION HAS TERMINATED       **
ECHO **              YOU HAVE RETURNED TO THE DOS PROMPT          **
ECHO ON
F6 Key or Ctrl Z
```

You now have in your DOS directory the batch file BIGBACK. This file performs a complete backup after you provide some start-up information. If you want to verify the file, use the TYPE command to send the file to the screen or use redirection to print the file.

A Batch File To Display Help Text

Using the batch-file provisions of DOS does not mean that you can only include commands that do DOS jobs. You can also include commands that provide information for you or another user. In this example, text information is echoed to the screen. The text provides help for the COPY

10

207

command. You can substitute your own help text for another DOS command using the same method.

This batch file is called COPYHELP.BAT. If you include it in your current directory, you can see the text by typing COPYHELP. Type the file as follows:

```
ECHO OFF
CLS
ECHO ************* COPY COMMAND HELP INFORMATION*********************
ECHO * FULL SYNTAX:                                                 *
ECHO *                                                              *
Echo * COPY sd:\path\filename.ext dd:\path\filename.ext /switches   *
ECHO *    sd=source drive letter, dd=destination drive letter       *
ECHO *    /V=Verify switch                                          *
ECHO *                                                              *
ECHO * A space separates source and destination file parameters.    *
ECHO *                                                              *
ECHO *          FILES ARE COPIED FROM SOURCE TO DESTINATION.        *
ECHO * ? wild card matches any character and * matches all.         *
ECHO *  Wild cards allow copying all files matching command line.    *
ECHO *                                                              *
ECHO *                   —COPY EXAMPLES—                            *
ECHO * (1)COPY A:*.* C: (2)COPY \TEMP\MYFILE.123 \KEEP\YOURFILE.XYZ *
ECHO * (3)COPY MEMO.DOC MEMO.BAK (4)COPY CON AUTOEXEC.BAT (re-       *
ECHO * direction using COPY CON)                                    *
ECHO *                                                              *
ECHO *****************************************************************
ECHO ON
```

Lessons Learned

■ Batch files are simple, but powerful, programs in the form of text files.

■ Batch files personalize your computer to your own wishes.

■ Batch files are the nonprogrammer's programming language, using DOS commands instead of programming code.

■ The AUTOEXEC.BAT file is always executed by DOS after CONFIG.SYS to make your computer operate more efficiently.

■ The CONFIG.SYS file configures your PC.

Now let's review some common DOS commands.

Common Commands and Your PC

DOS Commands by Purpose

Use this guide to determine the command you need in order to accomplish a specific task. Then refer to the the command listing that follows this list for details about the use and syntax of the command.

If You Want To ...	Use
Back up a hard disk	BACKUP
Concatenate files	COPY
Change the current directory	CHDIR (CD)
Change the current disk drive	*d:*
Change the date	DATE
Change the name of a file	RENAME (REN)
Change the time	TIME
Clear the screen	CLS
Compare disks	DISKCOMP
Compare files	COMP (and FC in MS-DOS only)

If You Want To ...	Use
Copy between devices	COPY, XCOPY
Copy disks	COPY, DISKCOPY, XCOPY
Display a text file on the screen	TYPE
Display batch file commands and text strings on the screen	ECHO
Display the amount of memory	CHKDSK
Display the contents of a file	TYPE
Display the date	DATE
Display the files on a disk	DIR, CHKDSK, TREE
Display the free space on a disk	CHKDSK, DIR
Display the subdirectories on a disk	TREE, CHKDSK
Display the time	TIME
Display the version of DOS	VER
Display the volume label	VOL, DIR, CHKDSK
Erase a character	Left arrow or ◆Backspace
Fix a file	CHKDSK, RECOVER
Locate a string in a file	FIND
Make a new directory	MKDIR (MD)
Move a file	COPY
Pause the display	Ctrl-S, MORE
Place DOS on the disk	FORMAT /S, SYS
Pipe the output between programs	|
Prepare new disks	FORMAT
Prepare the hard disk	FDISK, FORMAT
Redirect the input of a program	<, |
Redirect the output of a program	>, >>, |
Remove a file	ERASE, DELETE (DEL)
Remove a directory	RMDIR (RD)
Restore backed-up hard disk files	RESTORE
Set alternative directories for programs	PATH

11

If You Want To ...	Use
Set/change checks on file writing	VERIFY
Set/change the system prompt	PROMPT
Sort a file	SORT
Use a new device	DEVICE (CONFIG.SYS)

This chapter is a Command Reference, encompassing the most frequently used MS-DOS commands. Each command is presented in the same format:

1. The command name appears first, followed by the notation

   ⁎ Internal   or   External

   These graphics indicate whether the command is built into MS-DOS (internal) or is disk-resident (external).

2. The command's purpose is explained, followed by the syntax required to invoke the command.

3. A set of step-by-step instructions for using the command appears.

4. There will be a brief commentary stressing the emphasis you should place on mastering each command. Here, you will also be cautioned about any traps that apply to a particular command.

External Commands

You recall that DOS's internal commands may be issued from any disk drive or directory. Issuing external commands is a bit more complex. To issue an external command, you have three alternatives:

1. Change to the directory that holds the external command. These are best kept in a subdirectory containing all the other DOS files. On hard disks, the path is usually C:\DOS*filename*.

2. Include the path name (disk drive, if necessary, and directory name) each time you issue the command. This technique can quickly become tedious.

3. Make sure that the directory holding the external command is included in the last PATH command you issued.

11

If your AUTOEXEC.BAT file contains a PATH statement that includes the subdirectory holding the DOS files, external commands will be executed upon issuance.

If you issue a command and get a `Bad command or file name` message, you either don't have the path set with the PATH command, or else the command is not in the default directory on the logged disk drive. Remember the rule of currents for issuing commands:

1. If you do not give a disk drive name for the command, MS-DOS will search for the command on the current disk drive.

2. If you do not give a path, MS-DOS will search for the command in the current directory of the current disk (or the current directory of the specified disk drive if one was given).

A Note about Notation

In the command notation used in this chapter, *d:* is the name of the disk drive holding the file, and *path* is the directory path to the file. *filename* is the root name of the file, and *.ext* is the file name extension.

If any part of this notation does not appear in the syntax for the command, the omitted part is not allowed in that command. For example, the notation *d:filename.ext* indicates that path names are not allowed in the command.

Commands that use source and destination drive parameters use *sd:* for the source drive name and *dd:* for the destination (target) drive name. The *s* and *d* parameters are also used for other commands in some instances.

11

BACKUP

 External

Use BACKUP to:

Back up hard disk information to protect original programs and data in case of loss or damage.

Back up files created or altered since a specific date or since the last backup.

Copy long files that cannot be stored on one floppy disk.

Command Syntax

BACKUP *sd:spath\sfilename.ext dd: /switches*

Follow These Steps

1. Type **BACKUP** and press the space bar once. You may need to precede the command with a drive and path for BACKUP.COM because BACKUP is an external command.

2. Type the drive name of the hard disk to be backed up (*sd*). For example, type **C:** if you are backing up drive C. To back up only a directory or an individual file, type the path, file name, and extension; then press the space bar. You can use wild-card characters (* and ?) to designate groups of files.

3. Type the name of the drive that will receive the backup files (*dd*). For example, if you are backing up on a floppy disk in drive A, type **A:**.

4. Use any of the following optional switches with the BACKUP command:

   /S backs up the subdirectories as well as the current directory. If you start at the root directory, DOS will back up all subdirectories.

   /M backs up files modified since the last backup. Use the /A switch with the /M switch to avoid erasing unmodified files when restoring from the backup disks. These switches are used in incremental backups.

11

213

/A adds files to the files already on the backup disk.

/D: mm-dd-yy instructs DOS to back up files created or changed on or after a particular date.

/T: hh:mm:ss instructs DOS to back up files created or changed at or after a particular time (V3.3 and later).

/F formats the target floppy disk (V.3.3 only).

5. Press Enter.

Caution: Prior to backing up your files, remember to number the floppy disks you will use. If you should need to use the RESTORE command to restore lost files, the disks will be asked for in numeric order.

Backing up your hard drive reduces the chance that you will lose valuable information. It is not necessary for you to memorize every step, but you should become familiar with BACKUP's basic command and switches.

11

CHDIR or CD

| ✳ | Internal |

Use CHDIR or CD to:

Change the current directory.
Show the name of the current directory.

Command Syntax

CHDIR *d:path*

or

CD *d:path*

Follow These Steps

1. Type **CHDIR**. CHDIR (CD) is an internal command that does not require a path.
2. Press the space bar.
3. Type the drive name of the disk whose current directory is to be changed (for example, **A:**, **B:**, **C:**, etc.) and the name of the directory you want to change to. If you don't specify a path, the current path will be displayed. Remember to use the backslash to separate the parts of the path.
4. Press Enter.

CHDIR is a very important and simple command to use. This is one of the commands you need for navigating around your disk.

11

CHKDSK

 External

Use CHKDSK to:

Check the directory of the disk for disk and memory status. CHKDSK can show:

- the number of files and directories on a disk
- the bytes used and the space available on a disk
- the presence of hidden files
- whether a floppy disk is bootable
- the total RAM and available RAM
- whether files are fragmented (noncontiguous)

CHKDSK also can make minor repairs.

Command Syntax

CHKDSK *d:path\filename.ext* /F/V

Follow These Steps

1. Type **CHKDSK** and press the space bar. You may need to precede the command with a drive and path for CHKDSK (the optional *d:path* in the syntax), because CHKDSK is an external command.

2. To check a disk on another drive, type the drive name, followed by a colon, after CHKDSK. If your default drive is A, and you want to check drive B, type **CHKDSK B:**.

3. You can use CHKDSK to determine the noncontiguous areas in an individual file by entering the path, file name, and extension. The filename and extension can contain wild cards.

4. Specify optional switches:

    /F repairs errors (use with caution).

    /V = verbose, and displays paths and file names.

5. Press Enter.

11

Tip: CHKDSK informs you if the files on your disk are contiguous. It does not repair noncontiguous files. Placing the /F switch will repair the error—in theory. Frequently, CHKDSK will gather the fractured files and combine them in one special file in your Root Directory.

This simple command makes you feel more in control of your computer. It offers a quick analysis of your floppy and hard disks and should be issued once a week.

11

CLS

※ Internal

Use CLS to:

Clear the screen whenever you are at the DOS prompt.

Command Syntax

CLS

Follow These Steps

1. Type **CLS**.
2. Press Enter. After all messages on-screen are cleared, the DOS prompt and the cursor reappear in the upper left corner.

Including CLS is an excellent way to give your batch files a professional look. It's something to remember.

11

COPY

Use COPY to:

Copy one or more files to another disk or directory, or copy a file to the same directory and change its name.

Transfer information between DOS system devices.

Send text to the printer.

Create ASCII text files and batch files.

Command Syntax

The most common syntax for the COPY command is

COPY *sd:\path\filename.ext dd:\path\filename.ext /switches*

Follow These Steps

1. Type **COPY** and press the space bar.
2. Type the optional drive name and path of the source file (*sd:\path*).
3. Type the name of the file to be copied. Wild cards are allowed.
4. You can include the following switches for the source file:

   /A treats the source file as an ASCII text file.

   /B forces the entire file to be copied as though it were a program file (binary). Binary copying is the default value.
5. Press the space bar.
6. Type the optional drive name, path, and file name of the target file (*dd:\path*). Skip this step if the file name is to remain the same as that of the source file.
7. You may include the following switches for the target file.

   /A places a Ctrl-Z (end-of-file character) at the end of the copied file.

   /B prevents a Ctrl-Z from being added to a copied file.

11

219

8. You may add a /V switch to verify and check the accuracy of the COPY procedure.

9. Press Enter.

Caution: COPY does exactly what you ask of it. Before you use this command, make sure that you have planned well. If you are copying to another directory or disk, COPY will overwrite a file of the same name. Make certain that what you want is what you type, and this includes directory names.

COPY is a very flexible command that you should know like the palm of your hand.

11

DATE

 Internal

Use DATE to:

Enter or change the system date.

Set the internal clock on Personal Computer ATs and PS/2 computers.

Ensure the current date-stamp for newly created and modified files.

Provide control for programs that require date information, such as BACKUP and RESTORE.

Command Syntax

DATE *date_format*

Follow These Steps

1. Type **DATE** and press the space bar.
2. Enter the date in one of the three following formats:

   mm-dd-yy (for North America; this is the default)

   dd-mm-yy (for Europe)

   yy-mm-dd or *yyyy-mm-dd* (for East Asia)

   mm is a one- or two-digit number for the month (1 to 12).

   dd is a one- or two-digit number for the day (1 to 31).

   yy is a one- or two-digit number for the year (80 to 99). The 19 is assumed.

   yyyy is a four-digit number for the year (1980 to 2099).

   You can separate the entries with hyphens, periods, or slashes.
3. Press Enter.

If your PC doesn't have a built-in calendar clock, you should use this command every time you boot. It's good organizational strategy to know when files were written or updated. Better still, cards containing battery-operated calendar clocks have become very inexpensive of late. You can purchase one to eliminate typing the time and date every time you start your computer.

11

DEVICE

| ⟍ | Internal |

Use DEVICE to:

Support add-on peripherals.

Install a block-device driver.

Install a virtual (RAM) Disk.

Command Syntax

DEVICE= *device driver filename*

Follow These Steps

1. Using a text editor, open your CONFIG.SYS file. If you do not have a CONFIG.SYS file, create one with COPY CON or with a text editor.

2. Type on one line in your CONFIG.SYS file the command DEVICE= *device driver filename.*

3. Repeat Step 2 until all desired device drivers are included in your CONFIG.SYS file.

4. Restart your system.

Note: Device drivers usually come with hardware you purchase. Check installation instructions for your device and driver.

Sooner or later, you will add the DEVICE command to your CONFIG.SYS file. When you include the proper DEVICE commands, the command(s) are issued automatically every time you boot.

11

DIR

Internal

Use DIR to:

Display a list of files and subdirectories in a disk's directory.

List a specified group of files within a directory.

Examine the volume identification label of the disk.

Determine the amount of available space on the disk.

Check the size of individual files.

Check the date the files were last modified.

Command Syntax

DIR *d:\path\filename.ext* /W/P

Follow These Steps

1. Type **DIR** and press the space bar.
2. You can also type

    The drive name whose directory you want displayed;

    The path name whose directory you want displayed;

    The file name if you want to limit the number and types of files to be listed. You can use wild cards to list groups of files.
3. Specify optional switches:

    /W displays the directory in a wide format of five columns across. Only the directory name and file names will be displayed. For large listings, you can also include the /P switch.

    /P displays the directory and pauses between screen pages. This switch prevents large directories from scrolling past the screen before you can read them.
4. Press Enter.

11

223

DISKCOMP

 External

Use DISKCOMP to:

Compare two floppy disks on a track-for-track, sector-for-sector basis to see whether their contents are identical.

Verify the integrity of a DISKCOPY operation.

Command Syntax

DISKCOMP *source d: destination d:*

Follow These Steps

Dual Disk Drives

1. Type **DISKCOMP** and press the space bar.
2. Type the name of the drive that holds the source disk. For example, type **A:** and press the space bar again.
3. Type the name of the drive that holds the target disk (for example, **B:**).
4. Press Enter, and you will be instructed to place the source disk into drive A and the target disk into drive B.
5. Insert both disks and press Enter again. DISKCOMP compares all tracks and issues any necessary error messages, indicating the track number and side of the disk where errors occur. When DISKCOMP has finished, you will be asked whether you want to compare more disks.
6. Press Y or N. If you press Y, repeat steps 4, 5, and 6.

Single Disk Drive

1. Type **DISKCOMP**.
2. Press Enter. A prompt will appear instructing you to place the source disk in drive A.

11

224

3. Insert the source disk and press Enter once more. After a minute or two, a second prompt will instruct you to insert the target disk into drive A:.

4. Insert the target disk and press Enter again.

5. Continue swapping disks as prompted until DOS finishes comparing the disks. When the comparison is complete, you will be asked whether you want to compare another disk.

6. Press either Y or N. If you press Y, repeat Steps 2, 3, and 4.

Tips: Occasionally, when you check a disk containing .EXE files, an error message —End of file marker not found— may appear. Also, you can't use DISKCOMP with hard disks or RAM disks.

Many experienced users never use this command. It's an insurance policy, issued for problems that may never happen. However, if DISKCOMP makes you feel more secure, use it.

11

DISKCOPY

 External

Use DISKCOPY to:

Secure data against loss by duplicating a floppy disk. Note that DISKCOPY works only when copying floppy disks of the same size and capacity.

Command Syntax

DISKCOPY *source d: destination d:*

Follow These Steps

Dual Disk Drives

1. Type **DISKCOPY** and press the space bar.
2. Type the name of the drive that holds the source disk (**A:**, for example). Press the space bar once more.
3. Type the name of the drive that holds the target disk (**B:**, for example).
4. Press Enter. Within a few seconds, you will be prompted to place the source disk into drive A and the target disk into drive B.
5. Insert both disks and press Enter.
6. When the copy is complete, you will be asked whether you want to copy another disk.
7. Press either Y or N. If you press Y, repeat Steps 4, 5, and 6.

Single Disk Drive

1. Type **DISKCOPY**.
2. Press Enter. Within a few seconds, you will be prompted to place the source disk in drive A.
3. Insert the source disk and press Enter. After a minute or two, you will be prompted to insert the target disk.

11

4. Place the blank target disk into drive A and press Enter.

5. Repeat Steps 3 and 4 until DOS finishes copying. You will then be asked whether you want to copy another disk.

6. Press either Y or N. If you press Y, repeat Steps 2 through 4.

Tip: DISKCOPY is used for duplicating floppy disks, not hard disks. If a problem exists on the original (source) disk, the same problem will appear on the duplicate disk.

DISKCOPY is one of the basic commands that should be understood completely.

11

ECHO

 Internal

Use ECHO to:

 Display batch-file commands and text strings on the screen.

 Control video output to the screen.

 Debug batch files.

Command Syntax

To turn off the display of commands when you run batch files:

 ECHO OFF

To turn on the display of commands:

 ECHO ON

To display a message:

 ECHO *message*

ECHO is an excellent batch-file creation utility. If you understand its use, you can have a good deal of fun personalizing your PC's operation.

11

ERASE or DEL

| ✳ | Internal |

Use ERASE or DEL to:

Remove one or more files from the directory.

Command Syntax

ERASE *d:path\filename.ext*

or

DEL *d:path\filename.ext*

Follow These Steps

1. Type **ERASE** or **DEL** and press the space bar.
2. Type the drive name and path of the file to be deleted, unless the file is in the current directory.
3. Type the name of the file to be deleted.
4. Press Enter.

Caution: ERASE is a deceptively simple command that can make your life easy or fill it with grief. Practice using this command, and think carefully before hitting that Enter key. Be very careful when you are using wild cards, or you could easily delete more files than you intend.

11

229

FIND

 External

Use FIND to:

Display lines that contain, or fail to contain, a certain character grouping. These characters are called a string.

Command Syntax

FIND /C/N/V "string" *d:path\filename.ext*. . .

Note that switches for FIND are placed in the middle of the command line, before the search string is specified.

Follow These Steps

1. Type **FIND** and press the space bar. Note that the FIND filter is an external file. FIND's location (disk drive and path) may need to precede the FIND command if FIND is not in the root directory or on a path governed by the PATH command.

2. Specify optional switches:

   /C counts the number of lines that contain the string being searched.

   /N displays the line number of each line that contains the string.

   /V displays lines that do not contain the search string.

3. Type the string, enclosed in double quotation marks ("string"). The string is the character set you want FIND to search for. FIND is case-sensitive. If you want to find uppercase characters, for example, the "string" must be typed in uppercase letters.

4. If the file is not in the current directory, type the drive name and path where the file being searched is located.

5. Type the file name and extension of the file to be searched.

6. Press the space bar and repeat Steps 4 and 5 for each file you want FIND to search. You cannot use wild-card characters (? or *).

7. Press Enter.

FIND is a very convenient command, particularly important as your hard drive fills with numerous files and subdirectories.

11

FORMAT

External

Use FORMAT to:

Initialize a floppy disk or hard disk to accept DOS information and files.

Command Syntax

FORMAT *d:* /S /1 /8 /V /B /4 /N:*xx* /T:*xx*

Follow These Steps

1. Type **FORMAT**.
2. Press the space bar.
3. Type the name of the drive that will hold the floppy disk to be formatted. For drive B, type **B:**.
4. Select optional switches:

/V gives the formatted disk a unique, identifying volume label.

/S produces a bootable floppy disk with the DOS operating system on the formatted disk.

/4 formats, on a high-capacity drive, a single- or double-sided floppy disk to be used in computers that use double-density disks.

/1 formats a disk on one side. Use this switch to format minifloppy disks for older PCs and compatibles.

/8 formats a floppy disk with eight sectors per track instead of the default value of nine sectors per track. Use to format disks for older PCs and compatibles.

/B creates an eight-sector floppy disk that will reserve space for the operating system.

/N:*xx* formats a disk with a different number of sectors than the default value. xx represents the number of sectors. Always use this switch with the /T:*xx* switch.

11

231

/T:*xx* specifies a different number of tracks to format. xx represents the number of tracks. Use this switch with the /N:*xx* switch.

5. Press Enter.

6. DOS now instructs you to place a floppy disk into the drive you named in Step 3. Insert the disk to be formatted and press Enter.

7. In one to two minutes, you will see the message Format complete and a status report of the formatted disk.

8. If you selected the /V switch, you will be asked to enter the volume label, a name of 11 characters or fewer. Type the volume label and press Enter.

9. DOS then asks if you want to format another disk.

10. Press Y and repeat Steps 6 through 9 to format another disk. Or, press N.

Caution: If you format a 360K floppy disk in a 1.2M disk drive, it cannot always be read in a 360K drive. Also, a 1.2 M disk might look exactly like a 360K disk, but the higher density 1.2M disk cannot be used in a 360K disk drive.

An absolute must to understand, FORMAT is the heart of your disk-maintenance system.

11

MKDIR or MD

| ✳ | Internal |

Use MKDIR to:

Create subdirectories to help organize your files.

Command Syntax

MKDIR *directory specifier*

or

MD *directory specifier*

Follow These Steps

1. Type **MKDIR** and press the space bar.

2. You can also type the drive name and path of the new directory.

3. Type the directory name.

4. Press Enter.

If you have a hard disk drive, you should understand this command. It creates the "book shelves" for categorizing your files.

11

233

MORE

 External

Use MORE to:

Display data one screen at a time. Video output pauses between pages, and the message `--More--` is displayed. Press any key to display the next 23 lines of data.

Command Syntax

d:path\filename.ext | MORE

Depending on your intended use of MORE, you may need to precede the syntax with a program name that will act on the file name. For example,

TYPE *filename.ext* | **MORE**.

Follow These Steps

1. Type the name of the file you want displayed in groups of 23 lines and press the space bar.
2. Type the pipe symbol (|) and press the space bar.
3. Type **MORE** and press Enter.
4. Press any key to see more text displayed.

MORE is very convenient for reading files longer than one screen.

11

PATH

 Internal

Use PATH to:

Access files not in the default directory, without changing directories. PATH tells DOS to search specified directories on specified drives if a program or batch file is not found in the current directory.

Command Syntax

PATH *d1:\path1;d2:\path2;d3:\path3;. . .*

Follow These Steps

1. Type **PATH** and press the space bar.
2. Type the optional drive name to be specified in the search path— for example, **A:**, **B:**, or **C:**. If you include the drive name with the path, DOS will find your files, even if you change default drives.
3. Type the directory path to be searched—for example \ **KEEP**.
4. Then type:

   A semicolon if you are going to add another directory to the search path.

   The drive name and path of the additional directory to be specified in the search path.
5. Repeat Step 4 until you have completed typing all the subdirectory paths you want DOS to search.
6. Press Enter.

11

This is an important navigational aid whose use should be fully understood. If you don't understand PATH, you don't understand the directory concept.

235

PROMPT

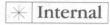 Internal

Use PROMPT to:

Customize the DOS system prompt.

Display the drive and directory path.

Display a message on the computer.

Display the date and time or the DOS version number.

Command Syntax

PROMPT *promptstring*

Follow These Steps

1. Type **PROMPT** and press the space bar.
2. Type the text string and arrangement of parameters you want.
3. You can use the meta-string characters, preceded by the dollar sign ($) with the PROMPT command to produce your own DOS prompt:

Meta-string	Characters
D	the current date
G	the > character
L	the < character
N	the current disk drive name
P	the current drive and path
Q	the = character
T	the system time
V	the DOS version
Any other	the character is ignored

Once it is placed in your AUTOEXEC.BAT with the desired information, you may never refer to the PROMPT command again. PROMPT is most frequently used to extend the visual command line to show the path of the current directory.

11

REN

 Internal

Use RENAME to:

Change the name of a file or group of files.

Command Syntax

RENAME *d:path\oldfilename.ext newfilename.ext*

Follow These Steps

1. Type **RENAME** or **REN** and press the space bar.
2. Type the optional drive name and path of the file to be renamed.
3. Type the file name of the file to be renamed. Wild-card characters (* and ?) may be used to specify groups of files.
4. Press the space bar.
5. Type the new name you want assigned to the file and press Enter.

Caution: It is a good policy to avoid giving files in different directories the same file names. You might accidentally delete the wrong file by mistake.

Practice with this one. It has a million and one uses.

11

RESTORE

 External

Use RESTORE to:

Retrieve one or more files from a backup disk and store on another disk, usually a hard disk.

Command Syntax

RESTORE *sd: dd:\dpath\dfilename.ext /switches*

Follow These Steps

1. Type **RESTORE** and press the space bar.
2. Type the name of the source drive that contains the backed up files. For example, type **A:** to restore files from drive A. Press the space bar.
3. You can type the name of the destination drive to receive the backup files. For example, if you are restoring files to a hard disk in drive C, type **C:** If you omit the drive name, the default drive becomes the destination drive.
4. Type the path (directory name) if you are going to restore files from only one directory.
5. Type the name and extension of the file or files you want to restore. You can use wild-card characters to designate a group of files. For example, type *.* to designate restoration of all files on a disk or subdirectory.
6. Specify optional switches:

   /S restores all files in the current directory and subdirectories of the current directory, creating subdirectories when necessary.

   /P elicits a screen prompt that asks whether you want to restore files that changed since the last backup or are designated by the ATTRIB command as read-only.

11

/M restores only files modified or deleted since the last backup.

/N restores only files that no longer exist on the target disk.

/B:mm-dd-yy restores only those files modified on, or before, a specified date.

/A:mm-dd-yy restores only those files modified on, or after, a specified date.

/L:hh:mm:ss restores files that have changed at, or later than, a specified time.

/E:hh:mm:ss restores files that have changed at, or earlier than, a specified time.

7. Press Enter. At the prompt, place a backup disk into the source drive and press Enter once more.

8. Repeat Step 7 until all the backup disks have been processed.

Tip: Remember, store your numbered disks in the proper order. The RESTORE operation can be crucial, and you don't want to create unnesessary complications in the middle of restoring files to your hard disk.

RESTORE is the flip side of the coin for BACKUP. Both should be understood equally well.

11

RMDIR or RD

 Internal

Use RMDIR to:

Remove a directory.

Command Syntax

RMDIR *d:path*

or

RD *d:path*

Follow These Steps

1. Use the ERASE command to delete any files from the directory to be removed. A directory must be empty to be removed. Only the current (.) and parent (..) files may remain in the directory.
2. Type **RMDIR** or **RD** and press the space bar.
3. Type the optional drive name of the directory to be removed.
4. Type the full path and name of the subdirectory to be removed.
5. Press Enter.

RMDIR is another essential to maintaining a logical hard disk drive subdirectory system.

11

SORT

 External

Use SORT to:

Read input data, sort it, and write it to an output device.

Sort and list directory information.

Display, arrange, and sort data alphabetically in ascending or descending order.

Command Syntax

SORT /R /+*n*

Follow These Steps

1. Type **SORT** and press the space bar.
2. Specify optional switches:

   /R sorts in reverse alphabetical order.

   /+ followed by an integer representing a column number sorts in alphabetical order, starting at the specified column.
3. Press Enter.

   Example: SORT /R <PRESORT.TXT >POSTSORT.TXT

   SORT will sort, in reverse alphabetical order, the contents of the PRESORT.TXT. The sorted contents will be written to the file POSTSORT.TXT.

SORT is not an essential command, but one of the niceties used for visual control.

11

241

SYS

 External

Use SYS to:

Transfer the operating system files to another disk. SYS permits the transfer of operating system files to a disk that holds an applications program if there is space for the additional files.

Follow These Steps

1. Place the target disk (the disk to receive the operating system) into a disk drive.
2. Type **SYS**.
3. Press the space bar.
4. Type the name of the target drive that holds the disk to receive the operating system, for example, **B:**.
5. Press Enter. SYS will transfer the operating system to the floppy disk in the target drive.
6. If you want to make a bootable system disk, follow the SYS command with the COPY command. If your system disk is in drive A, and your target disk is in drive B, type **COPY A:COMMAND.COM B:**.

Tip: It is not necessary to transfer the operating system to every floppy disk. Save disk storage space and only use SYS on disks you wish to use as a boot disk.

11

242

TIME

 Internal

Use TIME to:

Enter or change the time used by the system.

Set the automatic clock on Personal Computer ATs and PS/2 computers (beginning with DOS V3.3).

Establish the time files were newly created or modified.

Provide control for programs that require time information, such as BACKUP and RESTORE.

Command Syntax

TIME hh:mm:ss.xx

Follow These Steps

1. Type **TIME** and press the space bar.
2. Enter the time in the format *hh:mm:ss*, or in the format *hh.mm.ss*. For *hh*, type the hour, using one or two digits ranging from 0 to 23 hours. For *mm*, type the number of minutes in one or two digits ranging from 0 to 59. For *ss*, type the number of seconds in one or two digits ranging from 0 to 59.
3. To show hundredths of a second, you can press the period (.) and enter one to two digits from 0 to 99.
4. Press Enter.

To be used with the DATE command. Maybe it's not as important to place the correct time on a file, but don't get into poor management habits. Better still, think about getting a battery-powered clock card for your PC. The cost is small, and it saves time.

11

TREE

 External

Use TREE to:

Display directory paths in hierarchical directories.

Optionally list the available files in each directory.

Find lost files within a maze of directories.

Command Syntax

TREE *d: /F*

Follow These Steps

1. Type **TREE** and press the space bar.
2. Type the name of the drive whose directory paths are to be displayed. The TREE command will list information pertaining to this drive.
3. You may include the following switch:

    /F lists the files in each directory.
4. Press Enter.

The TREE command is another way to visually monitor a hard disk drive's directory structure. As time goes on, you'll appreciate it more.

11

244

TYPE

| ✳ | Internal |

Use TYPE to:

Display the contents of a text file on the screen.

Send files to the printer.

Command Syntax

TYPE *d:path\filename.ext*

Follow These Steps

1. Type **TYPE** and press the space bar.
2. Type the optional drive name, path, and file name of the file to be displayed.
3. Press Enter.

Note: Use the redirection symbol > to send the typed output to a device, such as the printer (PRN).

Example:

TYPE TEXT.TXT > PRN

TYPE is a real convenience for reading a text or batch file without using a word processor.

11

245

VER

 Internal

Use VER to:

Display the DOS version number.

Command Syntax

VER

Follow These Steps

1. Type **VER**
2. Press Enter. The version number will appear on the screen along with a message like this one:

```
IBM Personal Computer DOS Version 4.0
```

Pretty to look at, but infrequently used. Singularly limited in purpose.

11

VERIFY

| ✳ | Internal |

Use VERIFY to:

Set your computer to check the accuracy of data written to a disk.
Show whether the data has been checked.

Command Syntax

To show whether VERIFY is on or off, use

VERIFY

To set the verify status, use

VERIFY ON

or

VERIFY OFF

Follow These Steps

1. Type **VERIFY** and press the space bar.
2. Type **ON** or **OFF** depending on whether you want VERIFY on to check for accuracy or off for fast disk-writing operation.

VERIFY provides absolute peace of mind, but takes twice as long to copy files. Many people are in the habit of using verification. If you have the time, it just might be worthwhile.

11

247

VOL

 Internal

Use VOL to:

Display the volume label of the specified drive.

Command Syntax

VOL *d:*

Follow These Steps

1. Type **VOL** and press the space bar.
2. Before you press Enter, you may type the drive name of the disk whose volume name you want to examine (for example, **A:**, **B:**, etc.), if that disk is not in the current drive.
3. Press Enter.

Some people never use this feature but, in fact, it's as important as labeling a disk.

11

Errors Great and Small

U ntil appreciation of slapstick humor began to wane, one of the standard routines involved slipping on a banana peel.

What was funny? Certainly, not the fall. Everyone falls at one time or another, often with unpleasant results. Maybe the humor is there because nobody really gets hurt. You know the actors don't injure themselves. That's why an audience can sit back and enjoy the physical levity.

Before you finish this chapter, you'll realize that, while some of the DOS error messages are no laughing matter, it is possible that you will never see these kinds of errors appear on your screen. In fact, most of the common error messages allow us to smile at mistakes that we can easily correct.

What are Error Messages?

Ending a book with a chapter on errors may make you wince, but don't lose heart. You can treat with a grin most of the common DOS error messages. Error messages are DOS's way of telling you that you (or DOS) made a correctable blunder. Error messages serve as reminders that both man and machine make mistakes.

Recognizing error messages

Assessing the importance of error messages

Interpreting error messages

Correcting error messages

Occasionally, you may issue harmless but incorrect commands, or forget to close the door on a disk drive. Now and then, we all slip up, and DOS quickly reminds us of our frailties. It's important that we learn from our mistakes.

How Serious Are Error Messages?

Some error messages indicate a serious problem. Fortunately, you may never get to see one of those messages.

Some potentially serious error messages may be caused by one of several problems. If you remain calm, you might be surprised to discover an easy remedy. Meanwhile, read through the following error messages. These messages are the ones that routinely appear on your screen. Disasters are rare, so enjoy your PC, confident that you have earned your wings.

Interpreting and Correcting Error Messages

The actual wording of common error messages differs for the various implementations and versions of MS-DOS. These differences are often as slight as punctuation and capitalization. At other times, the entire content of the message may differ. If you see a message that you cannot locate in this guide, refer to your computer's MS-DOS manual.

Some messages appear when you start MS-DOS, and some appear while you use your computer. Most start-up errors mean that MS-DOS did not start and that you must reboot the system. Most of the other error messages mean that MS-DOS terminated (aborted) the program and returned to the system prompt. For easy reference, the messages and their most common causes are listed in alphabetical order.

12

```
Bad command or filename
```

The name you entered is not valid for invoking a command, program, or batch file. The most frequent causes are the following: (1) you misspelled a name; (2) you omitted a needed disk drive or path name; or (3) you gave the parameters without the command name.

Check the spelling on the command line. Make sure that the command, program, or batch file is in the location specified (disk drive and directory path). Then try the command again.

Bad or missing Command Interpreter

MS-DOS cannot find the command interpreter, COMMAND.COM. MS-DOS does not start.

If you are starting MS-DOS, the message means that COMMAND.COM isn't on the boot disk, or that a version of COMMAND.COM from a previous version of MS-DOS is on the disk. Place in the floppy disk drive another disk that contains the operating system and then reboot the system.

After MS-DOS has started, copy COMMAND.COM to the original start-up disk so you can boot from that disk.

If this message appears while you are running MS-DOS, COMMAND.COM may have been erased from the disk and directory you used when starting MS-DOS, or a version of COMMAND.COM from a previous MS-DOS may have overwritten the good version. You must restart MS-DOS by resetting the system.

If resetting the system does not solve your problem, use a copy of your MS-DOS master disk to restart the computer. Copy COMMAND.COM from this floppy disk to the offending disk.

Bad or missing filename

MS-DOS was directed to load a device driver that could not be located, or an error occurred when the device driver was loaded. It might also mean that a break address for the device driver was out of bounds for the size of RAM in the computer. MS-DOS will continue its boot but will not use the device driver.

If MS-DOS loads, check your CONFIG.SYS file for the line DEVICE=filename. Make sure that you spell the line correctly and that the device driver is where you specified. If this line is correct, reboot the system.

12

If the message appears again, copy the file from its original disk to the boot disk and try booting MS-DOS again. If the error persists, contact the dealer who sold you the driver, because the device driver is bad.

Batch file missing

MS-DOS could not find the batch file it was processing. The batch file may have been erased or renamed. For MS-DOS V3.0 only, the disk containing the batch file may have been changed. MS-DOS aborts the processing of the batch file.

If you are using MS-DOS V3.0 and you changed the floppy disk that contains the batch file, restart the batch file and do not change the disk. You may need to edit the batch file so that you do not need to change disks.

If you renamed the batch file, rename it again, using the original name. If necessary, edit the batch file to ensure that the file name does not get changed again.

If the file was erased, re-create the batch file from its backup file if possible. Edit the file to ensure that the batch file does not erase itself.

Cannot load COMMAND.COM, system halted

MS-DOS attempted to reload COMMAND.COM, but the area where MS-DOS keeps track of available and used memory was destroyed, or the command processor was not found. The system halts.

This message may indicate that COMMAND.COM has been erased from the disk and directory you used when starting MS-DOS. Restart MS-DOS. If it does not start, the copy of COMMAND.COM has been erased. Restart MS-DOS from the original master disks and copy COMMAND.COM to your working disk.

Another possible cause for this message is that a faulty program may have corrupted the memory allocation table where MS-DOS tracks available memory. Reboot and then try running the same program that was in the computer when the system halted. If the problem occurs again, the program is defective. Contact the dealer who sold you the program.

12

Cannot start COMMAND.COM, exiting

MS-DOS was directed to load an additional copy of COMMAND.COM, but could not. Either the FILES= command in your CONFIG.SYS file is set too low, or you do not have enough free memory for another copy of COMMAND.COM.

If your system has 256K or more of RAM, and FILES is less than 10, edit the CONFIG.SYS file on your start-up disk and use FILES = 15 or FILES = 20. Reboot your DOS.

If the problem occurs again, you do not have enough memory in your computer, or you have too many programs competing for memory space. Restart MS-DOS again and do not load any resident or background programs you do not need. If necessary, eliminate unneeded device drivers or RAM-disk software. Another alternative is to increase the amount of random-access memory in your system.

Configuration too large

MS-DOS could not load itself because you specified too many FILES or BUFFERS in your CONFIG.SYS file.

Restart MS-DOS with a different disk and edit the CONFIG.SYS file on your boot disk. Lower the number of FILES and/or BUFFERS. Restart MS-DOS with the edited disk. Another alternative is to increase the random-access memory in your system.

Current drive is no longer valid

You have set the system prompt to PROMPT $p. At the system level, MS-DOS attempted to read the current directory for the disk drive and found the drive no longer valid.

If the current disk drive is set for a floppy disk, this warning appears when you do not have a disk in the disk drive. MS-DOS reports a Drive not ready error. You give the **F** command to fail (which is the same as A for abort), or the **I** command to ignore the error. Then insert a floppy disk into the disk drive.

12

253

An invalid-drive error also can happen if you have a networked disk drive that has been deleted or disconnected. Simply change the current disk to a valid disk drive.

Disk boot failure

An error occurred when MS-DOS tried to load itself into memory. The disk contained IO.SYS and MSDOS.SYS, but one of the two files could not be loaded. MS-DOS did not boot.

Try starting MS-DOS from the disk again. If the error recurs, try booting MS-DOS from a disk that you know is good, such as a copy of your MS-DOS master disk. If this attempt fails, you have a hardware disk drive problem. Contact your local dealer.

Drive not ready

An error occurred while MS-DOS tried to read or write to the disk drive. For floppy disk drives, the drive door may be open, the disk may not be inserted, or the disk may not be formatted. For hard disk drives, the drive may not be properly prepared, or you may have a hardware problem.

Error in EXE file

MS-DOS detected an error while attempting to load a program stored in an EXE file. The problem is in the relocation information MS-DOS needs to load the program. This problem can occur if the .EXE file has been altered in any way.

Restart MS-DOS and try the program again, this time using a backup copy of the program. If the message reappears, the program is flawed. If you are using a purchased program, contact the dealer or publisher.

Error loading operating system

A disk error occurred while MS-DOS was loading itself from the hard disk. MS-DOS does not boot.

Restart the computer. If the error occurs after several tries, restart MS-DOS from a floppy disk. If the hard disk does not respond (that is, if you cannot

12

run DIR or CHKDSK without getting an error message), your problem is with the hard disk. Contact your local dealer. If the hard disk does respond, use the SYS command to put another copy of MS-DOS onto your hard disk. You may need to copy COMMAND.COM to the hard disk also.

EXEC failure

MS-DOS encountered an error while reading a command or program from the disk, or the CONFIG.SYS FILES= command has too low a value.

Increase the number of FILES in the CONFIG.SYS file of your start-up disk to 15 or 20 and then restart MS-DOS. If the error recurs, you may have a problem with the disk. Use a backup copy of the program and try again. If the backup copy works, copy it over the offending copy.

If an error occurs in the copying process, you have a flawed floppy disk or hard disk. If the problem is a floppy disk, copy the files from the flawed disk to another disk and reformat or retire the original floppy disk. If the problem is the hard disk, immediately back up your files and get assistance in running RECOVER on the offending file. If the problem persists, your hard disk may have a hardware failure.

File creation error

MS-DOS or a program attempted to add a new file to the directory or replace an existing file, but failed.

If the file exists, it may be a read-only file. If it is not a read-only file, run CHKDSK without the /F switch to determine whether the directory or the disk is full, or if another problem exists with the disk.

File not found

MS-DOS could not find the file you specified. The file is not on the disk or in the directory you specified, or you misspelled the disk drive name, path name, or file name. Check these possibilities and try the command again.

12

General failure

This is a catchall error message. The error usually occurs when you use an unformatted floppy disk or hard disk or when you leave the disk drive door open.

Incorrect MS-DOS version

The copy of the file holding the command you just entered is from a different version of MS-DOS.

Get a copy of the command from the correct version of MS-DOS (usually from the MS-DOS master disk) and try the command again. If the floppy disk or hard disk you are using has been updated to hold new versions of the MS-DOS programs, copy those versions over the old ones.

Insert disk with \COMMAND.COM in drive d and strike any key when ready

MS-DOS needs to reload COMMAND.COM, but can not find it on the start-up disk.

If you are using floppy disks, the disk in drive A has probably been changed. Place a disk holding a good copy of COMMAND.COM in drive A: and press a key.

Insert disk with batch file and strike any key when ready

MS-DOS is attempting to execute the next command from a batch file, but the disk holding the batch file isn't in the disk drive. This message occurs for MS-DOS V3.1. MS-DOS V3.0 gives an error message when the disk is changed.

Put the disk holding the batch file into the disk drive and press a key to continue.

12

Insufficient disk space

The disk does not have enough free space to hold the file being written. All MS-DOS programs terminate when this problem occurs, but some non-DOS programs continue.

If you think that the disk has enough room to hold this file, run CHKDSK to see whether the floppy disk or hard disk has a problem. Sometimes when you terminate programs early by pressing Ctrl-Break, MS-DOS is not allowed to do the necessary clean-up work. When this happens, disk space is temporarily trapped. CHKDSK can "free" these areas.

If you have simply run out of disk space, free some disk space or use a different floppy disk or hard disk. Try the command again.

Insufficient memory

The computer does not have enough free RAM to execute the program or command.

If you have loaded a RAM-resident program like SideKick or ProKey, restart MS-DOS and try the command before loading any resident program. If this step fails, remove any unneeded device driver or RAM-disk software from the CONFIG.SYS file and restart MS-DOS again. If this action fails, your computer does not have enough memory for this command. You must increase your random-access memory to run the program.

Invalid COMMAND.COM in drive d

MS-DOS tried to reload COMMAND.COM from the disk in drive d and found that the file was of a different version of MS-DOS. You will see a message instructing you to insert a disk with the correct version and press a key. Follow the directions for that message.

If you frequently use the disk that was originally in the disk drive, copy the correct version of COMMAND.COM to that disk.

Invalid COMMAND.COM, system halted

MS-DOS could not find COMMAND.COM on the hard disk. MS-DOS halts and must be restarted.

12

COMMAND.COM may have been erased. Restart the computer from the hard disk. If you see a message indicating that COMMAND.COM is missing, that file was erased. Restart MS-DOS from a floppy disk and recopy COMMAND.COM to the root directory of the hard disk.

If you restart MS-DOS and this message appears later, a program or batch file may be erasing COMMAND.COM. If a batch file is erasing COMMAND.COM, edit the batch file. If a program is erasing COMMAND.COM, contact the dealer who sold you the program.

Invalid directory

One of the following errors occurred: (1) you specified a directory name that does not exist; (2) you misspelled the directory name; (3) the directory path is on a different disk; (4) you didn't give the path character (\) at the beginning of the name; or (5) you did not separate the directory names with the path character. Check your directory names, ensure that the directories do exist, and try the command again.

Invalid disk change

The disk in the 720K, 1.2M, or 1.44M disk drive was changed while a program had open files to be written to the disk. You will see the message Abort, Retry, Fail. Place the correct disk in the disk drive and type **R** for Retry.

Invalid drive in search path

One specification you gave to the PATH command has an invalid disk drive name, or a named disk drive is nonexistent.

Use PATH to check the paths you instructed MS-DOS to search. If you gave a nonexistent disk drive name, use the PATH command again and enter the correct search paths. Or you can just ignore the warning message.

Invalid drive specification

This message is given when one of the following errors occurs: (1) you entered the name of an invalid or nonexistent disk drive as a parameter to a command; (2) you gave the same disk drive for the source and destination, which is not permitted for the command; or (3) by omitting a parameter, you defaulted to the same source and destination disk drive.

Certain MS-DOS commands temporarily hide disk drive names while the command is in effect. Check the disk drive names. If the command is objecting to a missing parameter and defaulting to the wrong disk drive, explicitly name the correct disk drive.

Invalid drive specification
Specified drive does not exist,
or is non-removable

One of the following errors occurred: (1) you gave the name of a nonexistent disk drive; (2) you named the hard disk drive when using commands for floppy disks only; (3) you omitted a disk drive name, and defaulted to the hard disk when using commands for floppy disks only; or (4) you named or defaulted to a RAM-disk drive when using commands for a true floppy disk drive.

Remember that certain MS-DOS commands temporarily hide disk drive names while the command is in effect. Check the disk drive name you gave and try the command again.

Invalid number of parameters

You have given either too few or too many parameters to a command. One of the following errors occurred: (1) you omitted required information; (2) you excluded a colon immediately after the disk drive name; (3) you put a space in the wrong place or omitted a needed space; or (4) you omitted a slash (/) in front of a switch.

Invalid parameter
Incorrect parameter

At least one parameter you entered for the command is not valid. One of the following occurred: (1) you omitted required information; (2) you forgot a colon immediately after the disk drive name; (3) you put a space in the wrong place or omitted a needed space; (4) you didn't add a slash (/) in front of a switch; or (5) you used a switch the command does not recognize.

12

259

Also check this message under the individual command for more information.

Invalid path

One of the following errors has occurred to a path name you have entered: (1) the path name contains illegal characters; (2) the name has more than 63 characters; or (3) one of the directory names within the path is misspelled or does not exist.

Check the spelling of the path name. If needed, get a directory listing of the disk to ensure that the directory you specified does exist and that you have the correct path name. Be sure that the path name contains 63 characters or fewer. If necessary, change the current directory to a directory "closer" to the file and shorten the path name.

Lock violation

With the file-sharing program (SHARE.EXE) or network software loaded, one of your programs attempted to access a file that is locked. Your first choice is **Retry**. Then try **Abort** or **Fail**. If you choose abort or fail, however, you will lose any data in memory.

Memory allocation error
Cannot load COMMAND, system halted

A program destroyed the area where MS-DOS keeps track of in-use and available memory. You must restart MS-DOS.

If this error occurs again with the same program, the program has a flaw. Use a backup copy of the program. If the problem persists, contact the dealer or program publisher.

Missing operating system

The MS-DOS hard disk partition does not have a copy of MS-DOS on it. MS-DOS does not boot.

12

Start MS-DOS from a floppy disk. If you have existing files on the hard disk, back up the files. Issue **FORMAT/S** to put a copy of the operating system on the hard disk. If necessary, restore the files that you backed up.

Non-System disk or disk error
Replace and strike any key when ready

Your floppy disk or hard disk does not contain MS-DOS, or a read error occurred when you started the system. MS-DOS does not boot. If you are using a floppy disk system, put a bootable disk in drive A and press a key.

The most frequent cause of this message on hard disk systems is that you left a nonbootable floppy disk in drive A, with the door closed. Open the door to disk drive A and press a key. MS-DOS will boot from the hard disk.

No paper

The printer is either out of paper or is not turned on.

Non-DOS disk

The disk is unusable. You can abort and run CHKDSK on the disk to see whether any corrective action is possible. If CHKDSK fails, your only alternative is to reformat the disk. Reformatting, however, will destroy any remaining information on the disk. If you use more than one operating system, the disk was probably formatted under the operating system you're using and should not be reformatted.

Not enough memory

The computer does not have enough free random-access memory to execute the program or command.

If you loaded a RAM-resident program, such as SideKick or ProKey, restart MS-DOS and try the command again before loading any resident program. If this method fails, remove any unneeded device driver or RAM-disk software from the CONFIG.SYS file and restart MS-DOS.

If this option fails, your computer does not have enough memory for this command. You must increase your RAM to run the command.

12

Not ready

A device is not ready and cannot receive or transmit data. Check the connections, make sure that the power is on, and check to see whether the device is ready.

Path not found

A file or directory path you named does not exist. You misspelled the file name or directory name, or you omitted a path character (\) between directory names or between the final directory name and file name. Another possibility is that the file or directory does not exist where you specified. Check these possibilities and try again.

Path too long

You gave a path name that exceeds the 63-character limit of MS-DOS. Either the name is too long, or you omitted a space between file names. Check the command line. If the phrasing is correct, change to a directory that is closer to the file you want. Try the command again.

Program too big to fit in memory

The computer does not have enough memory to load the program or command you invoked.

If you have any resident programs loaded (such as SideKick), restart MS-DOS and try the command again without loading the resident programs. If this message appears again, reduce the number of buffers (BUFFERS=) in the CONFIG.SYS file and eliminate unneeded device drivers or RAM-disk software. Restart MS-DOS. If these actions do not solve the problem, your computer lacks the memory needed to run the program or command. You must increase the amount of RAM in your computer to run this command.

Read fault

MS-DOS was unable to read the data, usually from a hard disk or floppy disk. Check the disk drive doors and be sure that the disk is properly inserted.

12

Sector not found

The disk drive was unable to locate the sector on the floppy disk or hard disk platter. This error is usually the result of a defective spot on the disk or of defective drive electronics. Some copy-protection schemes also use this method (a defective spot) to prevent unauthorized duplication of the disk.

Seek

The disk drive could not locate the proper track on the floppy disk or hard disk platter. This error is usually the result of a defective spot on the floppy disk or hard disk platter, an unformatted disk, or drive electronics problems.

Syntax error

You phrased a command improperly: (1) you omitted needed information; (2) you gave extraneous information; (3) you put an extra space in a file name or path name; or (4) you used an incorrect switch. Check the command line for these possibilities and try the command again.

Unable to create directory

Either you or a program attempted to create a directory, and one of the following errors occurred: (1) a directory by the same name exists; (2) a file by the same name exists; (3) you tried adding a directory to a root directory that is full; or (4) the directory name has illegal characters or is a device name.

Do a directory listing of the disk. Make sure that no file or directory already exists with the same name. If you are adding the directory to the root directory, remove or move (copy and then erase) any unneeded files or directives. Check the spelling of the directory and ensure that the command is properly phrased.

Unrecognized command in CONFIG.SYS

MS-DOS detected an improperly phrased directive in CONFIG.SYS. The directive is ignored, and MS-DOS continues to start. Examine the CONFIG.SYS file, looking for improperly phrased or incorrect directives. Edit the line, save the file, and restart MS-DOS.

12

Write fault

MS-DOS could not write the data to this device. Perhaps you inserted the floppy disk improperly, or you left the disk drive door open. Another possibility is an electronics failure in the floppy or hard disk drive. The most frequent cause is a bad spot on the disk.

Write protect

The disk is write-protected.

12

Installing DOS

U se the disks that came in the DOS package to make a working copy of DOS. Use the working copy with your computer and store the original DOS disks in a safe place.

Before you insert any disks from your DOS package into a drive, write protect the original disks. Cover the write-protect notches of 5 1/4-inch floppy disks with an adhesive, opaque tab. (In some cases, the write-protect notch on 5 1/4-inch disks is not cut: these disks are permanently write-protected.) 3 1/2-inch floppies have a write-protect window with a sliding shutter that must be open for the disk to be write-protected.

There are several versions of DOS. Various vendors of computers use specific instructions that pertain only to their versions of DOS. Check your DOS manual for instructions that may apply your version of DOS. The general instructions in this appendix allow you to make a working copy of DOS on a floppy disk for use with this book. Remember to use the disks that came in your package only to create working copies of your original disks, not as a working DOS disk!

Installing MS-DOS, Versions 3.3 and earlier

Installing DOS Version 4.XX

Floppy and hard disk considerations

Installing MS-DOS Versions 3.3 and Earlier

Versions of DOS up to V3.3 usually contain a DOS system disk and a supplemental files or diagnostics disk. You will need the DOS system disk for this operation. To make a bootable working disk, you will do the following:

1. Boot your computer using the DOS system disk.
2. Copy the DOS system disk to a new floppy disk.
3. Label the new floppy disk.

Booting with the DOS System Disk

Locate your DOS system disk and insert it into drive A. Turn the computer on. If it is already on, press and hold down the Ctrl and Alt keys and press the Del key. Your computer will boot from the DOS disk. Booting will take from a few seconds to a couple of minutes. When your computer beeps and displays screen information, read the display. If the message NON SYSTEM DISK or an equivalent message appears, you have chosen the wrong disk from your DOS package. Repeat this procedure with the correct disk. If you are prompted for the date and time, enter the current date and time. When the computer displays the DOS prompt (almost always A>), your system is successfully booted.

Copying the DOS System Disk

The disk-copying operation makes a working copy of your system disk. If your package has a system disk 1 and a system disk 2, you will need to repeat this operation to copy both disks. You can optionally repeat this operation to make a working copy of the DOS supplemental or diagnostics disk or other disks from your package. In all cases **insure that the DOS package disks are write protected**.

From the keyboard, type **DISKCOPY** and be sure to press Enter. DOS will prompt you to insert a disk or disks. Follow the sequence DOS leads you through. When DOS refers to the *source* disk, you will insert the DOS system disk from your DOS package into the drive specified. When DOS refers to the *target* disk, insert the blank disk into the drive DOS specifies. Depending on your system's memory and the number of drives you have, the DOS messages

A

to insert disks will vary. Because the DOS system disk is write-protected, you will be safe from accidental insertion of the wrong disk. When the disk copy operation for the disk is complete, DOS will ask if you want to make another copy. Answer **Y** for yes if you want to copy the other disks in the DOS package. Answer **N** for no if you have just one system disk to copy. When you have finished copying the disk(s) and answer N to the prompt, DOS redisplays the A> prompt.

Labeling the Copies

Remove all disks from the drives. Place a label on the DOS working disk, being careful not to touch the disk's internal surface. To write on a disk's label, use a felt-tipped pen. Never use a ball point pen or a pencil. If you must use a ball point pen, write on the label *before* putting it on the disk. If it is a 5 1/4-inch disk, put the disk back into its jacket. Put the original DOS disks back in their holders for safe storage away from heat, moisture, and electrical fields.

Label the copy of the system disk "DOS Working Master." If you made additional disks from your package, label them now, using the "Working" description along with the name on the original disk. Since you will use the working DOS disk to learn DOS commands, there is a chance that you could erase the disk. For additional safety, you should write-protect the working copy now.

To test the working DOS disk, insert it into drive A. Press Ctrl, Alt, and Del together to warm boot your system. The computer will display the DOS prompt again, and you can proceed with the exercises in this book.

Installing DOS V4.0

DOS V4.0 comes with an installation program called SELECT. The SELECT program can configure the DOS Shell to suit your computer's configuration. SELECT allows you to install DOS V4.0 on floppy disks or on a hard disk. The following procedure shows you how to create working copies of DOS V4.0 on floppy disks. You can then use the working copies with examples in this book.

A

267

Note that PC DOS V4.0 is an operating system designed specifically for IBM computers and may not work satisfactorily on other computers.

Memory Requirements for DOS V4.0 Installation

To install DOS V4.0, your computer must have at least 256K of random-access memory (RAM). If your system has less, ask your dealer about options to upgrade your memory. DOS V4.0's DOS Shell will be fully installed if you have at least 360K of RAM.

Floppy Disk Installation

If you are installing DOS V4.0 on 5 1/4-inch disks you will need the five 5 1/4-inch 360K disks that came with your DOS V4.0 package and four blank 5 1/4-inch 360K disks to create working copies.

If you are installing DOS on a 3 1/2-inch 1.44M disk, you will need the two 3 1/2-inch 720K disks that came with your package and one blank 3 1/2-inch 1.44M disk to create the working copy.

If you are installing DOS on a 3 1/2-inch 720K disk, you will need the two 3 1/2-inch 720K disks that came with your package and two blank 3 1/2-inch 720K disks to create the working copies.

The disks that came with the package must be write protected. For 3 1/2-inch disks, open the write-protect shutter. For 5 1/4-inch disks, cover the write-protect notch with an adhesive write-protection tab. The original 5 1/4-inch DOS disks are normally write protected permanently.

Special Key Assignments for Installation

SELECT uses some of your keyboard keys for special purposes during installation. Press F1 and then F9 to see a reminder of these special key assignments. The following table summarizes the special keys in SELECT.

268

Table A.1
Special Key Assignments for Installation

Key	Function
Tab	Moves the cursor to the next choice.
Arrow keys	Move the cursor in the direction of the arrow key.
Enter	Takes you to the next step. (Be sure to read information presented by SELECT first.)
Esc	Takes you back to the preceding SELECT screen. Information typed on the current screen is not saved.
PgUp PgDn	Move through HELP information when it is displayed.
F1	Brings help information to the screen. During certain operations, help is not available.
F3	Discontinues the installation process.
F9	Shows special key assignments when you view Help.

Running SELECT

To install DOS V4.0 onto 360K floppies, begin by labelling four blank disks "Startup," "Shell," "Working 1," and "Working 2." If you are installing DOS onto 720K floppies, label the two blank disks "Startup" and "Shell." If you are installing DOS onto a 1.44M floppy disk, label the new disk "Startup." These new disks should *not* be write protected at this time. Make sure, however, that your original disks are write protected.

Insert the DOS V4.0 INSTALL disk in drive A. Now press and hold down the Ctrl and Alt keys, and then press Del. If your system's power is off, turn the power on instead. This step reboots your computer and starts the SELECT program.

SELECT presents an opening identification screen and asks you to press Enter to continue. If, for some reason, you don't want to continue, press Esc now. If you elect to continue, SELECT asks you to pick the drive where you want to install DOS. Depending on your hardware, this drive could be A, B, or the hard disk C. For this installation, select A or B. Use the up- or down-arrow keys to highlight your selection. Press Enter.

A

269

During SELECT's operation, you will be asked to switch disks several times. Confirm the disk's identity by checking its label before you proceed. SELECT is designed to pick options on the installation screens that correspond to your computer's configuration. You will be safe letting SELECT make its choices. Any choices will be highlighted, and you can select them by pressing Enter.

Once the installation process is complete, remove the DOS original V4.0 disks and store them in a safe place. The Startup disk that SELECT created will be your working DOS disk. If you have a 360K floppy system, some of the DOS external commands may be found on the Working 1 and Working 2 disks.

SELECT creates two files, AUTOEXEC.400 and CONFIG.400. You can rename them AUTOEXEC.BAT and CONFIG.SYS at a later time. The two files tailor the way your computer starts and configures. You learn more about these files in Chapter 10.

To view the files that reside on the working disks, use the DIR /W command (Chapter 4). Any working disk that shows the file COMMAND.COM will start DOS from drive A. Normally, the Startup disk will serve as your working DOS disk. The Shell disk will start the DOS Shell. You can exit the Shell at any time and go to the DOS prompt to do the exercises in this book.

Hard Disk Installation

CAUTION: If you do not know how to prepare your hard disk, you could accidentally select an installation option that would cause permanent loss of data from your hard disk. This section on hard disk installation is intended for experienced users. Please use caution.

You can optionally run the installation operation to install V4.0 onto your hard disk, but you should follow certain precautions before hard disk installation. If your computer is on a local area network (LAN), consult the network administrator before attempting to install V4.0 on your system. If you share backed up files with other computer users under the guidance of a lead user, ask the lead user to clarify the implications of BACKUP and RESTORE before proceeding with hard disk installation of V4.0.

If you bought your computer and DOS V4.0 from a dealer, ask the dealer to assist you with hard disk installation of DOS. If you currently have another

A

operating system installed on your hard disk, such as OS/2, XENIX, or UNIX, read and understand the IBM DOS V4.0 *Getting Started* manual's discussion. For hard disk installation of PC DOS 4.0, have ready one new or blank floppy disk that SELECT will use to record your configuration options during the installation.

If you are familiar with the DOS FDISK command and understand the implications of preparing a hard disk, follow the procedures for installing DOS 4.0 to a hard disk. If you do not know about FDISK, do not select hard disk installation from SELECT's options. SELECT does not require you to run FDISK, but SELECT does prompt you for selections which are based on the functions of FDISK.

SELECT optionally installs DOS 4.0 to your hard disk if a hard disk is detected. SELECT permits you to partition your hard disk automatically if it does not have a primary DOS partition.

SELECT then formats the hard disk after it has completed the partitioning step. Hard disks that are already partitioned before running SELECT are not partitioned again by SELECT if you allow SELECT to make its own choices at the prompts. If you have a new hard disk which has no partition on it, SELECT will volunteer this step as part of the installation process.

If your hard disk has already been partitioned and formatted, SELECT will copy the hidden system files to your hard disk from the DOS V4.0 disk. You can optionally specify a directory to hold the DOS V4.0 commands and utilities. By default, SELECT copies the commands and utilities as well as the Shell files to the \DOS directory. Any command or utility files with duplicate names in the directory you choose will be replaced during V4.0 installation.

SELECT detects hard disks that only need upgrading of the DOS version to 4.0. Except for changing the DOS files, SELECT leaves the existing file system intact if no partitioning or formatting of the hard disk is required.

Since DOS V4.0 supports partitions larger than 32M. Users who have hard disks with capacities greater than 32M may elect to remove existing partitions and install one large partition. This change will take advantage of V4.0's larger partition size capability. **Warning**: removing a partition will destroy the files in that partition.

The booklet, *Getting Started*, that comes in the PC DOS V4.0 package devotes many sections to hard disk installation. You should consider that booklet the source for additional information about installing PC DOS V4.0.

A

A

Index

* and ? wild-card characters, 84-86, 138, 151, 165, 213
/+ switch
    SORT command, 241
/1 switch,
    FORMAT command, 98, 231
/4 switch,
    FORMAT command, 97, 231
/8 switch,
    FORMAT command, 98, 231
< and > redirection symbols, 174-175, 245

A

/A switch
    BACKUP command, 163-164, 213-214
    COPY command, 219
/A:date switch
    RESTORE command, 164, 239
Alt key, 17
APPEND command, 101
applications programs, 34
    directories, 121
    running, 43-44
arrow keys, 16, 80
ASCII (American Standard Code for Information Interchange), 14
    text files, 170, 193, 219
ASSIGN command, 101
asterisk (*) wild-card character, 84-86, 138, 151, 213
    RESTORE command, 165
AUTOEXEC.400 file, 194, 270
AUTOEXEC.BAT file, 119-120, 188, 194-197, 198-202, 236, 270
    backing up, 200-201

entering new, 201-202
keeping several versions, 202
viewing, 199-200

B

/B switch
    FORMAT command, 98, 231
/B:date switch
    RESTORE command, 164, 239
Backslash (\) key, 110, 113, 117, 140
    as command delimiter, 80
Backspace key, 16, 80
BACKUP command, 101, 155, 159-164, 166-167, 183, 190, 209, 213-214
    /A switch, 163-164, 213-214
    /D switch, 163-164, 214
    /F switch, 161, 163-164, 214
    /M switch, 163-164, 213
    /S switch, 162-163, 213
    /T switch, 163-164, 214
backup files, 155, 159-168, 213-214
    and DOS versions, 168
    CHKDSK command, 183-184
    preparing floppy disks, 159-161
    restoring, 164-165, 238-239
Bad command or filename message, 250-251
Bad or missing Command Interpreter message, 251
Bad or missing filename message, 251-252
BAS file extension, 37
BASIC programming files, 37
BAT file extension, 37, 110, 189, 192-193, 196-197, 199
Batch file missing message, 252

Index

Unrecognized command in
 CONFIG.SYS, 263
Write fault, 264
Write protect, 104, 264
Esc (Cancel) key, 17, 80-81
EXE file, 254
EXE file extension, 37, 110, 174, 193, 196-197
Exec failure message, 255
executable program files, 37
expansion slots, 21
extended ASCII codes, 14
external commands, 73, 88, 101, 211-212

F

/F switch
 BACKUP command, 161, 163-164, 214
 CHKDSK command, 181-183, 216-217
 TREE command, 127-128, 244
FC (MS-DOS) command, 209
FDISK command, 210, 271
File creation error message, 255
file extensions, 83-84
 .BAS, 37
 .BAT, 37, 110, 189, 192-193, 196-197, 199
 .CLR, 37
 .COM, 36, 110, 174, 193, 196-197
 .CPI, 37
 .DAT, 37
 .EXE, 37, 110, 174, 193, 196-197
 .HLP, 37
 .MEU, 37
 .MOS, 37, 174
 .OVL, 174
 .PRO, 37
 .SYS, 37
File not found message, 255
File System screen, 61-64
files, 8, 22, 30, 38, 129-152
 ASCII text, 170, 193, 219
 AUTOEXEC.400, 194, 270
 AUTOEXEC.BAT, 119-120, 188, 194-202, 236, 270
 backup, 155, 159-168, 213-214
 BASIC programming, 37
 batch, 34, 37, 44, 188-196, 206-208
 BIGBACK.BAT, 207

binary, 174, 219
cannot be added to directory, 255
checking size, 223
color configuration, 37
command, 36
COMMAND.COM, 39-41, 44, 50, 73, 79, 119, 125, 189, 251-253, 255-258, 270
CONFIG.400, 270
CONFIG.SYS, 119, 188, 202-206, 222, 251, 253, 255, 257, 261, 263, 270
COPYHELP.BAT, 208
controlling, 130
copying, 85, 136-149, 219-220
 all in directory, 141-142
 device to disk, 172-173
 different directories, 147-148
 disks, 142-143
 floppy to hard disk, 145
 same directory, 146
 single file between disks, 144
data, 37
date/time stamp, 84, 196, 221
dates when modified, 223
deleting, 149-151
destination, 130
disk changed while open, 258
display screen operation, 37
displaying contents, 245
erasing, 79, 229
EXE, 254
executable program, 37
finding, 244
fragmentation, 130, 142, 184-185
full backup, 162-163
graphics-mode printer profiles, 37
help, 37
inactive, 120
input/output system, 39, 41
IO.SYS, 254
listing, 82-86, 223, 244
locked, 260
managing, 42
menu handling, 37
mouse operation, 37
MSDOS.SYS, 254
naming, 83-84
operating system unable to find, 255

Index

Using DOS
Developed by Que Corporation

The most helpful DOS book available! Que's *Using DOS* teaches the essential commands and functions of DOS Versions 3 and 4 —in an easy-to-understand format that helps users manage and organize their files effectively. Includes a handy **Command Reference**.

Order #1035
$22.95 USA
0-88022-497-5, 550 pp.

1-2-3 Release 2.2 QuickStart, 2nd Edition
Que Corporation

Quick guide to learning 1-2-3! Packed with illustrative examples and exercises, this text teaches readers how to develop and use spreadsheets, databases, and graphs on 1-2-3. Organized in modular sections that focus on the fundamentals of 1-2-3 and building 1-2-3 applications.

Order #1207
$19.95 USA
0-88022-612-9, 400 pp.

WordPerfect 5.1 QuickStart
by Que Corporation

Perfect beginner's guide to WordPerfect 5.1! This graphics-based text is a fast-paced introduction to the essential functions of WordPerfect. Hundreds of illustrations demonstrate document production, pull-down menus, table design, equation editing, file merging, and mouse support.

Order #1104
$19.95 USA
0-88022-558-0, 500 pp.

Windows 3 QuickStart
Que Corporation

This comprehensive tutorial teaches Windows beginners how to use the feature-packed Windows environment. With special emphasis on such software applications as Excel, Word, and PageMaker, Windows 3 QuickStart shows how to master the mouse, menus, and screen elements.

Order #1205
$19.95 USA
0-88022-610-2, 400 pp.